The Art of Coordinating Mind, Body and Brush

By William Reed

Japan Publications, Inc.

All photos, illustrations, and brushwork were prepared by the author or adapted from other sources, with the indispensable help of Sensei Kôshû Morioka (on Figs. 4-9, 5-4, 5-9, 5-14, 7-15, 7-17, 8-18, 8-19, 9-5, 9-7, 9-9, and others). In most cases, classic works could only be presented as excerpts, due to space limitations.

Photo Credits:
p. 23 (Fig. 1-1), *Zen and Japanese Culture*, Kubo Kinenkan Museum; p. 60 (Fig. 3-24), from 24th Sansô Shoten Calligraphy Exhibition, by permission of Minami Fujô Sensei; p. 77 (Fig. 5-1), *Ukiyoe*, Sadao Kikuchi, Hoikusha Publishing Co., 1964; p. 110 (Figs. 7-19, 7-20) and p. 141 (Fig. 9-13), *Kokuji to Gain Tzukuri*, Chô Yôseki, Japan Publications, Inc., 1986; p. 129 (Figs. 8-26, 8-27, 8-28), *A Japanese Touch for Your Garden*, Kiyoshi Seike, Masanobu Kudô, David Engel, Kodansha International, Ltd., 1980; p. 139 (Fig. 9-10) and p. 155 (Fig. 10-27), *The Design Heritage of Noren*, Tadashi Masuda, Graphic-sha Publishing Co., 1988; p. 140 (Fig. 9-12), from catalog, with permission from Nihon Meimon Shukai; p. 146 (Fig. 10-1), *Sake—A Drinker's Guide*, Hiroshi Kondo, Kodansha International, Ltd., 1984; p. 149–50 (Figs 10-10, 10-11, 10-12, 10-13), *Smaller Is Better*, O-Young Lee, Kodansha International, Ltd., 1982; p. 146-47 (Fig. 10-2, 10-5), *Kites, Crackers, and Craftsmen*, Camy Condon and Kimiko Nagasawa, Shufunotomo Co., 1974; p. 146(Fig. 10-3), *Sushi, A Light and Right Diet*, Asako Kishi, Japan Publications, Inc., 1983; p. 147-48 (Fig. 10-6), *Creative Origami*, Kasahara Kunihiko, Japan Publications, Inc., 1967; p. 148 (Fig. 10-7), *Gift Wrapping*, Kunio Ekiguchi, Kodansha International, Ltd., 1985; p. 148 (Fig. 10-8), *The Book of Kimono*, Norio Yamanaka, Kodansha International, Ltd., 1982; p. 148 (Fig. 10-9), *A Japanese Touch for Your Home*, Koji Yagi, Kodansha International, Ltd., 1982; p. 150 (Fig. 10-14), *Flower Arrangement Quick and Easy*, Shufunotomo Co., Ltd. 1971; p. 150 (Fig. 10-15b), *A First Zen Reader*, Trevor Leggett, Charles E. Tuttle Co., 1960; p. 151 (Fig. 10-16), *Designers Guide to Japanese Patterns*, Jeanne Allen, Kawade Shobo Shinsha Publishing Co., 1984; p. 151 (Fig. 10-17), *Textile Designs of Japan*, Japan Textile Color Design Center, 1959; p. 154 (Fig. 10-25), Tachibana-ryū Rakugo Script, written by Sakon Tachibana.

Published by JAPAN PUBLICATIONS, INC., Tokyo and New York

Distributors:
UNITED STATES: *Kodansha International/USA, through Farrar, Straus & Giroux, 19 Union Square West, New York, 10003.* CANADA: *Fitzhenry & Whiteside Ltd., 195 Allstate Parkway, Markham, Ontario, L3R 4T8.* BRITISH ISLES: *Premier Book Marketing Ltd., 1 Gower Street, London WC1E 6HA.* EUROPEAN CONTINENT: *European Book Service PBD, Strijkviertel 63, 3454 PK De Meern, The Netherlands.* AUSTRALIA AND NEW ZEALAND: *Bookwise International, 54 Crittenden Road, Findon, South Australia 5007.* THE FAR EAST AND JAPAN: *Japan Publications Trading Co., Ltd., 1–2–1, Sarugaku-cho, Chiyoda-ku, Tokyo 101.*

First edition: November 1989

LCCC No. 88–81760
ISBN 0–87040–786–4

Printed in U.S.A.

To Leah, for her love of living things,
Adria, for her creative imagination,
and
Benjamin, for his ready smile

Foreword

Most people remember one winter in the early 1980s, when an airliner plunged into the chilly Potomac River on its approach to the Washington National Airport. Rescuers repeatedly tossed lifelines into the water, in a effort to save those who could be saved in the few precious minutes that remained. One middle-aged man gave up his rope over and over again, so that the weaker passengers could go up first. But his own strength eventually failed him, and he himself drowned.

The Japanese papers carried this story as a noble example of the Western spirit. This story transcended the everyday news of economic concerns, and was beyond the domain of science and technology. The spirit of this man's selfless determination is difficult to explain in words, but its meaning was plain enough to be understood by people of any cultural background.

The spirit of a foreign culture is often difficult to understand, and does not lend itself to easy physical expression. Japan is an island nation which has a culture that is unique, even in the Far East. For much of its history it has developed in relative isolation from the rest of the world. This makes the Japanese people particularly difficult for outsiders to understand. To many people in other countries, the Japanese spirit is baffling and elusive.

The Japanese *Haiku* is the world's shortest poem. Though it is fairly well known overseas, in literal translation it is very difficult to understand. Bashô's famous *Haiku* reads:

> *Furu ike ya Kawazu tobikomu Mizu no oto*
> Old pond—Frog jump in—water sound.

Though in English, this appears to be nothing more than a mundane observation of a commonplace event, in Japanese its rhythm and imagery contain hints of an entire cultural tradition, and a profound view of the Universe based on Buddhist thought. Much of this becomes apparent when the poem is written with a brush.

In this book, William Reed has looked beyond the surface appearances of Japanese culture. I have great respect for his open-minded and unbiased efforts to understand the essence of Japanese culture, which he has pursued through extensive research into *Ki*, and its applications in the arts of *Aikido* and *Shodo*. I have enjoyed the opportunity of teaching Mr. Reed for a number of years now, and can say that he has looked long and well beyond the surface. In this book he has managed to write a comprehensive source on the art of Shodo, not from the perspective of a Japanese, but as a Westerner who has successfully penetrated the barriers of language and culture. The book is enjoyable, sensible, and well organized, and essential reading for anyone interested in gaining a deeper understanding of Japan.

Kôshû Morioka
Director of the Sôgei Kai Calligraphy Institute
September 1988 Tokyo, Japan

Preface

It was the Chinese who first said that a picture was worth a thousand words. In fact, Chinese and Japanese words are composed of legible pictures, called characters. Though bewilderingly complex to the untrained eye, these symbols embody an inner logic, a coherent psychology, and highly refined aesthetic qualities. But the complexity of Shodo, or Oriental brush writing, still confounds the Western mind. Not only in language, but in economics and politics as well, the barriers which separate East and West are real. But they are not as difficult to penetrate as usually assumed. What is required is a change in perspective, learning a new way to look at the unfamiliar.

Calligraphy is like music, with which it has much in common. Both can be enjoyed without learning to play the instrument. Each has a long tradition, including official, religious, classical, folk, and jazz styles. Both music and calligraphy involve reading and interpreting a score. Either can be enjoyed in recorded form or in live performance. Both involve a sense of rhythm, and depend on emotional expression as well as technique for their appeal. But one is visual, and the other auditory.

The Japanese have shown no hesitation in applying Western arts and skills to their own culture. We may equally benefit by seeing what of their culture might apply to ours. Educators, engineers, and designers have already begun to recognize the importance of visual thinking, and the close relationship between perception and creativity. Calligraphy does for the eye and the imagination, what music does for the ear and the soul. It is a sophisticated form of visual, tactile, and mental training. Shodo is not just for Orientals. Nor is it just for artists. It is for anyone interested in exploring alternative ways of thinking and creative problem solving.

Acknowledgments

The subject of mind and body coordination is covered in depth in an earlier book, *Ki: A Practical Guide for Westerners* (Japan Publications, Inc., 1986), which describes the principles of Ki energy, its expressions in Japanese culture, and practical applications in daily life. This book was based on a study of *Aikido* which I began in Japan in 1972, under Kôichi Tôhei, founder of the Ki Society International, and author of several books on Ki development. This experience led to an appreciation that the essence of the Japanese arts was not technique, but coordination of mind and body.

Suspecting that Ki principles might equally be applicable to the art of brush calligraphy, I decided to find out. I was extremely fortunate then, to have met Shodo Master Kôshû Morioka in 1983, just ten years after having begun training with Master Tôhei in Ki and *Aikido*. Though the terminology, techniques, and style of practice in calligraphy were quite different, I found it to be a kindred art with a comparable spirit. Mr. Morioka graduated from Tokyo University, where he trained as a psychologist. He took up calligraphy in the middle of his career, intrigued by what it seemed to reveal of the person behind the brush. He is now perhaps the top handwriting analyst in Japan, numbering among his clients many Japanese executives, police officers, and people from all walks of life. He was able to profile my personality quite accurately, having never met me, using nothing more than a sample of my handwriting on a postcard. This led to a personal meeting, after which I enrolled as a student in his calligraphy school. His kind and generous attention helped me to articulate what it was that I saw that was universal to the Japanese arts. The result was this book.

Starting anything new is an awkward experience. The newcomer is clumsy, makes foolish mistakes, and feels like a child in a grown-up world. The most difficult thing is relearning how to learn, going back to the beginning. It matters much less what you know at the moment, so long as you keep learning. The secret to creative growth in any field of endeavor is sustained and relaxed concentration. But how do you know if you are fully concentrated and relaxed? The results of your work tell how you did after the fact, but simply knowing how you did does not tell you how to approach the next attempt. Therefore each chapter ends with five concise principles which summarize aspects of the art. Still in all, the greatest principles are those which you will discover from your own experience.

It is difficult to properly acknowledge all of the people who have influenced one's thinking, but in the context of this book, two deserve special mention. The first is Dr. Betty Edwards, Professor of Art at California State University, and author of *Drawing on the Right Side of the Brain* (J. P. Tarcher, Inc., Los Angeles, 1979), whose original ideas on drawing and creative thinking provided me many clues about the art of brush calligraphy. The second is Dr. O-Young Lee, Professor of Literature at Ewha Women's University in Seoul, Korea, and author of *Smaller Is Better* (Kôdansha International, Ltd., Tokyo, 1984), whose brilliant analysis on Japan's mastery of the miniature was both inspiring and insightful in examining Japanese culture as a whole. Lectures and articles of Father Joseph R. De Roo, a scholar of the Chinese and Japanese writing system at St. Joseph's Friary in Tokyo, provided much helpful and detailed information on the etymology and rationale of the written characters. Certain ideas and illustrations on the psychology of perception were adapted from, *An Introduction to Psychology* (by Atkinson, Atkinson, Smith, and Hilgard, published in 1987 by Harcourt, Brace, Iovanovich). And of course there are dozens of books and people from whom I have drawn invaluable advice and guidance since 1 first came to Japan in 1972.

Introduction

Shodo is the art of Oriental brush calligraphy, that is painting Chinese or Japanese characters. The word Shodo means "Way of the Brush," indicating that it is as much a philosophy of living as an art form. However most books on calligraphy have little to say on this aspect, presenting instead details on the techniques of character writing. Practicing Shodo as a way of life does not mean earning one's living from it, or engaging in esoteric contemplative exercises. When properly used, the brush can help the student to integrate the mind and body. It not only renews the self within, but offers a visible trace of this renewal, in the form of balanced characters and well-executed strokes.

This can be a powerful tool in an age of alienation like the present. Alienation is a feeling of separation within. Urban life can cause us to feel cut off from nature. Working for a large and impersonal organization may cause us to feel cut off from other people. But neither of these is as alienating as the feeling of being cut off from one's self.

Although the purpose of education is to develop human potential, the achievements of genius remind us that few people use more than a fraction of that potential. It usually takes a crisis, within or without, to bring latent talent to the surface. In Japanese, a crisis (*kiki*) is known as a dangerous opportunity. If we focus on the negative aspects of a situation, then it defeats us. If we focus on the positive aspects, then it integrates our strength, and brings out the best in us. Alienation is a state of disintegration, which leaves a person powerless to deal with a crisis, large or small. To find the opportunities in a potentially dangerous situation requires an integration of all of our faculties, mental and physical.

The problem is that under pressure, we are likely to respond automatically, according to our subconscious habits. If we are accustomed to working, thinking, or playing at only a fraction of our potential, then we should not expect to do our best in a crisis. Most of our educational and work standards are set so low that daily life seldom provides the challenges necessary for growth. Though the opportunities may be available, there is not often much social support to pursue them. The only way to integrate and develop your latent strengths is to practice solving problems, until coordination of mind and body becomes second nature.

In other words, it is possible to improve yourself by practicing a discipline which is too difficult to take casually, yet tangible enough to provide feedback and practical results. This is the thinking behind many of the Zen inspired traditions of China and Japan, which have refined this process through many specialized branches of the arts: Zen archery and swordsmanship, the Noh theater, the tea ceremony, landscape gardening, ceramics, and calligraphy. These arts offer a way of integration to the mind which is divided from itself.

The feeling of separation, not only of mind and body, but of humanity from nature, has been traced in part to the unbridled advance of the analytical mind in the service of science and technology. Ironically, scientists on the frontiers of both physical and biological research have produced overwhelming evidence that there is no real separation of mind and body, or even of observer and observed. The distinction is artificial, and depends largely on where we choose to draw the line. Our brains apparently have a dual thinking capacity which allows us to make this distinction. We are equipped with a verbal, analytical, logical and linear left-brain, as well as a nonverbal, synthetic, spatial and holistic right-brain. The balanced use of both gives us a proper perspective on life. To overemphasize one or the other is to limit your outlook; to deny one or the other is to ignore reality.

In both East and West, the modern world is highly materialistic. People pursue that which they can see, grasp, or use. Put another way, people only have eyes for the obvious. Confucius said that if a man takes no thought about what is distant, he will find sorrow near at hand. Much of what eludes our conscious attention is just as real, and may be more important. If you can only see what everyone else sees, then you walk about with cultural blinders. The creative mind is more at home with the subtle and the unseen, because there are the contours of things to come. But the creative mind is not satisfied merely imagining things unseen; it is driven to make them visible. This is as true in the arts as it is in engineering, business, or any other field depending on creative endeavor.

Emerson reminded us that in every work of genius we recognize our own rejected thoughts. We ask ourselves, "Why didn't I think of that?" A more provocative question is, "Why didn't I do that?" Often, the reason we do not act on our creative impulses is that we lack the tremendous energy it takes to create. A person whose mind and body are divided lacks the concentration, intensity, and strength to create. Effective performance requires correct posture and a relaxed bearing, with the mind calm and focused on the task at hand. Slouching in a chair may provide relief from fatigue, but it also drains you of the motivation to act. Trying to do too many things at once may give you a feeling of activity, but a busy mind may be too scattered to be productive. Only when the mind and body are integrated and focused on the task at hand, is there enough creative energy to overcome the inertia of the divided self. Art gives us the discipline to develop this creative energy.

A Brief Note on Pronunciation:

Brush calligraphy is an art which originated in China. Both the Chinese and Japanese use written characters, but their pronunciation differs entirely. There are even regional differences in pronunciation within the same language. To avoid confusion, and because all of my study has been in Japanese, I have chosen to use the Japanese reading of the characters in almost all cases, including for the reading of Chinese names. Where needed the character is included in the text.

Pronunciation of Japanese words, which for the most part appear in italics, basically follows these simple rules:

a   as in calm
i   as in east
u   as in pull
e   as in net
o   as in solo

Pay attention to the difference between long (ô) and short (o) vowels, as this can change the meaning entirely. Double consonants are spoken with a slight pause in-between: *ippai* is pronounced ip-pai. There are other rules, but these are the important ones. As is conventional with common words like Tokyo, an exception has been made for the word Shodô (calligraphy), which appears so frequently that it is written here simply as Shodo.

Contents

18

20

Part I: The Readiness to Create

"The bee draws nectar from the flower, and produces honey. The silkworm chews the mulberry leaf, and produces a fine silken thread. Each consumes a nutrient, and produces something entirely different. In the same way, we must ingest the Calligraphy of the past, and create something of our own for the present. Only by transforming the work of others, can we create something uniquely our own."

Chapter 1

The Brush as an Extension of the Self

Calligraphy in Context

Fig. 1-1

Calligraphy is sometimes referred to as the last martial art. The famous Japanese medieval swordsman, Miyamoto Musashi, was also a master of the brush. His early seventeenth century painting of a shrike on a dead branch is pure presence of mind (Fig. 1-1). It is a visual representation of his teaching that the mind which sees the whole without stopping at the part, can reduce a dozen opponents to a single state of awareness.

Many famous martial artists and Zen priests were also excellent calligraphers. The brush magnifies the power of concepts which are difficult to put into words. The act of painting itself is intense and imme-diate, but it leaves a lasting trace, a vivid impression of the mind that produced it. One of the most difficult things in life to learn is how to integrate the mind and body, and apply one's fullest resources to the task at hand. We are too easily distracted from our goals. Tension and fear often get the best of us, and prevent us from realizing our full potential. There are people who are poised and single-minded in the face of difficulty, but this often seems to be an inborn trait. Exceptional people may be able to relax and perform well under pressure, but the average person finds it too difficult a task. The underlying purpose of many of the traditional Japanese arts is to learn how to calm the mind and rejuvenate the body, through constant discipline and practice in the techniques of the Way (*dô*). Shodo is the "Way of Brush Writing." For many people, stories of the hard training of Zen masters have made the Japanese arts esoteric and put them out of reach. The nuances of an aloof spiritual discipline can seem pretty remote from the pressing concerns of daily life. The practitioners of the arts have done little to help close the gap. By claiming that the arts are beyond words, or can only be known through experience, many popularizers of the

Zen school have cloaked them in secrecy. Few interpreters of the arts have been able to break the spell. The problem is compounded even further with Shodo, because calligraphy is often written in archaic scripts, or in highly cursive and abstract forms which are illegible even to modern Japanese. People on both sides of the language barrier assume that there is no point in pursuing something which you cannot read. Leonardo da Vinci said that all of our knowledge has its origin in our perceptions. The biggest challenge in the beginning is simply learning how to really look at what is written, and learning how to faithfully reproduce it with the brush. Later you become more creative, by learning how to reproduce what you see with the mind's eye. It is more important at first to learn how to look at Shodo, than to be concerned about exactly what it says. There are several approaches to overcoming the language barrier, which are explained in detail in later chapters.

It should be stated at the outset that you cannot master calligraphy by learning solely from a book. A serious student needs the benefits of personal feedback from a teacher. A book can introduce you to the subject however, help you get started, provide valuable information or references, and put the subject in personal perspective. The Oriental brush has much to teach us about the relationship between mind and body, perception and creativity, imagery and design, and even personality itself. We should take a long look at each of these topics, and then decide on the benefits of further study.

The primary feature of the brush (*fude*) which makes it difficult to control is that the bristles are soft. A Japanese proverb says that the soft overcomes the hard. Trying to control the brush with force is all but useless. The brush is so flexible and responsive that it accurately mirrors your own mental and physical attitude. Rigid thinking produces rigid brush strokes. The same principle operates in the throwing art of *Judo*, in which a smaller person can overcome a larger opponent by entering when pulled, and yielding when pushed. In both calligraphy and the martial arts, slackness is your undoing. A loose connection means poor communication and poor control. Trying to tame something with a will of its own is an extremely difficult task, because it does not respond in the way that you expect. When mind and body are unified, the eyes are calm and clear, the muscles quick and responsive. This quality is transmitted to the brush, and becomes visible in the brush strokes. Slackness reflects a discontinuity between mind and body, and results in poor control of the brush. The secret to mastering the brush is learning to take up the slack by relaxing the body, quickening the mind, and becoming versatile enough to lead rather than follow the brush.

An anonymous story of Zen origin illustrates the way to master the unmanageable self. A woodcutter at work was surprised by an unfamiliar creature in the forest. Wanting to catch it alive, he was startled when it spoke to him saying, "So you want to catch me alive?" He was astonished when it followed by saying, "You are surprised I can read your mind." Angered by the creature's impertinence, he thought to kill, rather than capture it. Again the beast responded, "Now you want to kill me, don't you?" Deciding to ignore the beast, the woodcutter resumed his work. But the animal persisted, "Now you've decided to neglect me." Finally the woodsman put the creature out of his mind, and fully concentrated on his work. At that moment, the axe flew off its handle and struck the chatterbox dead.

This tale was intended as a parable for *satori*, or enlightenment, but it is a good description of the learning process a student goes through in using the brush. In spite of your best efforts to control it, the brush seems to mock you and go its own way. We tend to be distracted by our own divided selves, until we learn to focus fully on the task at hand, and quiet the excess noise within.

Trying to solve the problem strictly by trial and error is too long and uncertain a process. Practice is necessary, but it should be guided by an understanding of how to use the brush. The principles which follow will give you a better understanding of how to control and use the brush as an extension of yourself.

Keep the Weight of the Body forward, and the Elbow down

Unlike Western painting with its vertical canvas, Oriental calligraphy is always done on a flat horizontal surface. A thin sheet of paper (*kami*) is stretched across a felt undercloth (*shita-jiki*), and held in place by hand or with paperweights (*bunchin*). The writing surface may be on the floor, or it may be on a table at about navel height. There are three basic postures in Shodo: you may sit on a chair, kneel on the floor, or stand up and bend over the paper. In all cases, the weight of the body should be forward, with the elbow bent at a natural angle. Many Shodo textbooks urge you to keep good posture by sitting erect. However if this is overemphasized, it brings the shoulders up and back, and puts the weight of the upper body on the spine. This makes the body artificially rigid, and forces the elbow to straighten out in order to reach the paper. Writing with a stiff arm makes it even harder to control the brush.

Good posture cannot be achieved by standing at attention in military style. A rigid posture is always unstable. Monkeys and four-legged creatures maintain stability by leaning forward. Using four limbs gives the animal more support, and keeps the body lower to the ground. Human beings stand erect, it would seem in a completely different posture from the four-legged creatures. Yet there is an important similarity between the two postures which is easy to overlook. The hind legs of a dog or horse bend at a point about half-way between the foot and the hip, and point back toward the tail. Its height off the ground makes it look like a backward pointing knee. However anatomically, this bend in the leg corresponds to the human heel, not the knee. As our evolutionary ancestors gradually stood erect, bringing the heel closer to the ground, the length of the bottom half of the leg grew progressively shorter. But the heel itself was never designed to take the weight of the upper body, nor was the spine. Whether bending forward or standing up straight, the weight of the body should fall on the front surface of the body, not the back.

Although the upper body leans forward at a slight angle to paint, the lower back should be firm and upright. Animals use a tail for balance, and the position of the tail tells a great deal about the animal's attitude. A cowardly dog tucks its tail between its legs, while a confident hunting dog will extend its tail like an antenna. Much the same thing happens with human beings, but there is not much tail to see. Keep the lower back erect, as if riding in a saddle, and the weight will naturally come forward.

Painting in an unstable posture results in weak and uncertain brush strokes. What happens when the weight falls back? In the standing position, the weight falls on the heels. If this posture becomes habitual, it eventually results in flat-footedness, and a corresponding state of mental lethargy. If the weight falls back in the seated posture, it puts pressure on the lower vertebrae of the spine, and gradually weakens the entire hip and abdominal region. Whether seated or standing, the weight of the upper body should fall on the lower abdomen in the front of the body. Leaning forward, the weight moves slightly to the front, but remains in the same general area. There is a remarkable difference in the stability of the body when the weight is forward and when it is back. You can test the difference very easily by having someone press steadily on your chest toward the rear with the fingertips of the hand. When the weight is forward the posture is as firm as a rock; when the weight settles back the body is easily unbalanced (Fig. 1-2).

Fig. 1-2

It may seem that leaning forward to paint would automatically distribute the weight properly, however this is not the case. Sitting in a chair, with both legs thrust out to the front, settles the weight on the spine rather than the abdomen. Only when you tuck the feet under the chair can you bring the center of gravity forward. The same effect can be achieved by sitting in the *seiza* posture, with the legs folded under (Fig. 1-3).

Fig. 1-3

When the writing surface is on the floor, you must stand or kneel above it. The exaggerated forward lean helps keep the weight in front, but straightening the knees automatically brings the weight up, and the center of gravity too far forward. Bending the knees lowers the hips and brings the weight down, but should not come back so far as to let the weight settle on the heels. There are no strict rules about how much to bend the knees. You are free to set one or

Fig. 1-4

both knees down on the floor. When you crouch down, you may need to raise the heels off of the floor and stand on the balls of the feet.

The direction of painting is from the top to the bottom of the page. In other words, you paint toward your feet. As long as the brush is in front of your knees there is no problem. But if you let the brush get too close to you, the weight may be forced up and you will feel top heavy. This means that you must take a step or two backward before you paint the next phrase, without losing concentration. By standing on the balls of the feet, you are always ready to move. If you stand flat-footed, you are more likely to get in your own way, and lose continuity when you move. The proper stance for the standing posture somewhat resembles the sprinter's ready position (Fig. 1-4).

The brush is held in the right hand, although being right-handed seems to offer no particular advantage. The position of the elbow is more important. Beginners tend to hold the elbow either too far out to the right, or too close in to the body. You can see why this is wrong by placing your left hand on the muscles of your left lower back, while moving the right elbow in a small circle, as if painting with the brush. If the elbow is too far out or too far in, then its circular movement causes the weight of the hips to shift from side to side, upsetting the center of gravity. When it is properly down and away from the body, it can move freely in any direction without disturbing the center of gravity. When the weight of the upper body is forward it falls on the lower abdomen. This area remains undisturbed like the eye of a hurricane, no matter how the arms and legs move. This calm center generates centrifugal force through the brush, which gives the strokes a clear and crisp quality.

Fig. 1-5

The elbow itself feels very heavy to lift when it is down, and very flimsy when it is out to the side. You can verify this for yourself while holding the brush, or by testing another person (Fig. 1-5). There is no need to push down or lean on the elbow to get this effect, it happens naturally when the weight is properly distributed. If the elbow is in the right position, it automatically corrects the hips. If the weight is properly distributed, the movement of the feet take care of themselves. There is less movement in the seated position than in standing, but the principle is the same.

Bend the Elbow, Not the Wrist

There are several major differences between painting with the brush and writing with a pencil. Fine details can be drawn with a pencil by articulating the small muscles in the wrist and fingers. It seems natural to assume that the brush could be manipulated in the same way. However the bristles of the Oriental brush are long and soft, while the tip of the pencil is rigid. The brush is designed like a miniature whip. A small movement of the handle produces a large movement of the tip, while a large movement of the handle takes all of the sting out of the whip. To maximize the energy of the bristles, the movement of the stem of the brush should be reduced to a minimum.

This does not mean that the stem is lifeless. A rapidly spinning top appears to be still, but this calmness is a result of rapid and highly refined movement. The stillness of the stem is deceptive, like the still, but rapidly moving wings of a dragonfly. It is almost impossible to produce this vibrant calmness if you bend the wrist and joints of the fingers as you would in writing with a pencil.

Fig. 1-6

Rather it is the elbow which bends, though it stays down and fairly level. The lower part of the wrist makes a convex curve, like a Japanese sword, and the palm is held facing down and forward (Fig. 1-6). The wrist in this position is very strong, and helps transfer the movement of the arm to the paper. If you bend the wrist, the palm turns in toward you, the elbow is pushed out and the balance of the body is broken. When this happens, the upper part of the abdomen grows tense, indicating that the weight has come up and back. Once the relationship between the wrist, elbow, and distribution of the weight is understood, it all becomes very simple. Keep the wrist unbent in the right position, and the stomach will stay relaxed, the weight will settle properly in the lower abdomen, and your arm will be free to move without interference. The elbow and wrist positions should become second nature, so that you can free your mind to concentrate on what you are painting, and still maintain control of the brush.

Keep the Stem Vertical and the Fingertips Pointed down

We are accustomed to holding most writing utensils on a diagonal. It feels awkward at first to hold the stem of the brush vertically, particularly if the elbow must be kept down at the same time. The balance of the brush, and consequently the control of the brush strokes, is lost when the stem is held on an angle. This is not to say that it never varies from the vertical, but like a figure skater, remains straight most of the time.

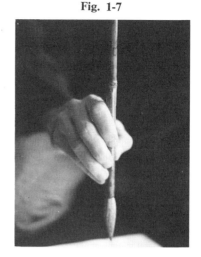

Fig. 1-7

Holding the brush upright is easy enough, but the fingertips must also point down, roughly perpendicular to the writing surface (Fig. 1-7). It is difficult to concentrate on the surface of the paper if the fingertips are pointing elsewhere off to the side or toward the wall, although some books actually recommend this. As there are various ways of holding a golf club, there are many alternate styles for holding the brush. It is even possible to develop a certain amount of skill despite a wrong grip. However, it makes sense that the fingers should point parallel to the stem of the brush, toward the paper where the mind is focused.

The hand position should be comfortable. Nevertheless, comfort alone will not guarantee that you get it right. O-gishi, the great Chinese calligrapher of the fourth century, explained that the brush should be poised vertically over the paper, the mind alert but relaxed, the palm cupped as if it were holding an egg against the stem of the brush. After so instructing his son, O-kenshi, he quickly grabbed the stem of the brush, and tried to snatch it from the boy's hand. When neither the brush nor the hand moved, he exclaimed that his son would undoubtedly become a great calligrapher. If the brush is held without concentration, it can be easily pinched from the fingers. But if the grip is too tense, then it inhibits the free movement of the arm. The image of holding an egg in the palm, without crushing it or letting it drop, creates the proper degree of concentration (Fig. 1-8).

Fig. 1-8

The tips of the fingers must be secure on the stem of the brush. If the stem is nestled in the first joint of the finger, rather than secured by the fingertip, the brush can easily be slipped from the hand. It is not necessary to pull on the stem with too much strength. If the grip is wrong, either the stem will slide or the hand will come up. It is a test of control, not a contest of strength (Fig. 1-9).

Control of the brush has much in common with the draw of a violin bow across its strings. Too much body movement or pressure, and you get only noise. This is sometimes misunderstood in avant-garde "performances" of calligraphy, in which large brushes, wild movement, and surprises like throwing the brush into the air,

Fig. 1-9

are used to impress audiences who are unfamiliar with the *dô* or "Way" of brush writing, which requires a more disciplined approach. In Shodo, the concept of "throwing away the brush," describes the breaking of the balance of the stem, leading to a brush stroke in which the energy of the line is suddenly broken.

O-kenshi once tried to secretly test his father, by rubbing out all but the faint outline of a piece of calligraphy which his father had painted on wood, and then painting it in again himself, trying to see if O-gishi would notice the forgery.

When his father returned, he looked at the piece, blinked his eyes, and said, "I must have been really drunk when I did this!" Control of the brush is so exquisite that even a master cannot forge another's hand beyond a few strokes. Control of the brush begins with a sure and undivided mind, and a vertical stem held fast in the fingertips.

Keep the Bristles Parallel and Untwisted

Some Shodo books teach to apply ink only to the tip of the brush. However, unless you fully saturate the brush, the dry bristles easily become twisted, and the brush becomes even harder to control. The upper part of the brush should contain ink, not air. You rarely paint with more than the tip of the brush, so the upper two-thirds of the bristles act as an ink reservoir. The saturated upper part of the brush helps keep the bristles parallel and allows you to paint many characters in sequence. If the upper part of the brush is dry, it will bend like a link in a chain, and break the firm connection between the tip and the stem (Fig. 1-10 a and b).

Fig. 1-10a

Fig. 1-10b

The brush operates most effectively when each of the hairs are relatively parallel. Each hair of the brush should taper to a point, so that the tips of as many hairs as possible can come in direct contact with the surface of the paper. This would be easy if the brush were just dragged along a straight line at a constant height. Of course this never happens in calligraphy. The brush is in constant motion, executing precise turns, negotiating narrow passages, and rising and falling with the thickness of the line. Only when the hairs are in rough alignment can a new stroke be executed cleanly. If the hairs become twisted and crossed, the brush becomes very awkward and unresponsive.

Fig. 1-11

The easiest way to maintain alignment is to avoid pressing down too hard on the paper. If the brush is saturated with ink, then a light amount of pressure causes the bristles to fan out and produce a thick line using only the tip of the brush. When the brush is only slightly lifted, the hairs draw in and taper to a point, producing a thin line. The tip of the brush

Fig. 1-12a

Fig. 1-12b

opens and closes like a fan (Fig. 1-11). This allows you to produce wide variations in the thickness of the line, and even to make many sharp directional changes without getting tangled up. If too much pressure is applied, the body of the brush bends, and the tips of the hairs are forced off of the surface of the paper. Not only does this take the sting out of the whip, but it leaves the brush hairs bent and unusable for the next stroke, and over time may damage the bristles. The proper amount of pressure causes the bristles to bend, but does not take away their elastic spring (Fig. 1-12 a and b).

Inevitably for the beginner, the brush does become bent and twisted. If this happens, you can readjust it by applying more ink, or by brushing the bristles lightly against the side of the ink dish. When not in use, the brush can be temporarily stored in a vertical brush stand (*fude-tate*), which will help keep the bristles moist, firm and aligned (Fig. 1-13). However if the brush is not going to be used for a few days, it should be washed to remove residual ink. If it is left unwashed for too long, the ink may become dried and encrusted, causing the bristles to bind and lose flexibility. A few drops of shampoo can help to clean the brush thoroughly.

Fig. 1-13

Paint with Controlled, Continuous Exhalation

The brush is a delicate and precise instrument. To use it properly requires full attention and good breath control. Though breathing is a natural process, it also reflects our mental and physical condition. The way a person breathes is often a clue to internal thoughts and feelings, and the depth and calmness of the breath is a good barometer of health. Breathing is usually so automatic that we hardly even notice it until we are anxious or have health trouble. The brush gives us a way to gauge and control the breath so that it works for and not against us.

If the movement of the brush is not coordinated with the breath, then the resulting line becomes weak and uncertain. What is the best way to steady the line? The flow of ink from the brush is very sensitive to the flow of breath from the lungs. The line on paper is like a silent voice in song. It is impossible to sing while inhaling, and much the same can be said about the brush. An opera singer can sustain a long phrase through steady and controlled exhalation, pause for only a moment, and then continue singing as though no inhalation were taken at all. There are far more notes in any piece of music than there are rests. It only takes a moment to fill the lungs when one has the proper posture. Breathing with the brush means maintaining the same quality of breath control, exhaling as you paint, and inhaling when the brush is between strokes. It is very difficult to paint a strong and steady line while inhaling. Controlled exhalation gives you a greater sense of awareness.

Even as the last ounce of breath is expelled, the singer must be ready to sing another phrase the next moment, without appearing hurried or out of breath. A singer who is winded at the end of a song is doing something wrong. In calligraphy, the beginner often finds the brush running out of ink after a single character. A skilled calligrapher can draw a column of six to ten characters without once refilling the brush. This is largely a matter of proper breath control.

It is not necessary to make the breath audible, or to try to hold or extend it beyond the limits of comfort. Practice and awareness will teach you how to breathe properly. It is more important to notice how steady, controlled exhalation improves the quality of the line, than to try to set any records.

Where to Concentrate the Mind

In the martial arts, beginning students find great difficulty dealing with an oncoming attacker. Even when the arm and footwork is known, somehow the opponent comes too fast to analyze or react appropriately. Naturally the movements become more automatic with practice, but there is no guarantee that a real attacker will approach or react in the same way. Textbook solutions are notoriously unreliable. Students are taught first to calm the mind by concentrating on the lower abdomen (*shita-hara*), and then to expand their awareness to embrace the entire situation. This is extremely difficult, because the mind wants to fix on some particular detail, such as the weapon, or some aspect of the technique in order to control the opponent. The problem with this is that it does not work. Serial awareness is simply too slow to deal with a spontaneous situation.

In calligraphy the opponent is oneself. You attempt to come to terms with the divided self by writing characters in perfect balance on paper, with a brush that magnifies and mocks your every move. Trying to concentrate on one feature of the character, your thought is reflected by a gross exaggeration of that feature on paper, out of proportion and missing the other elements. Trying to focus on one of the principles for controlling the brush, you may spoil the effect by being too self-conscious. The problem is like a Zen paradox, you are damned if you do, and damned if you do not. Where then should you concentrate the mind?

Although the brush should be held firmly in the fingertips, it is a mistake to think that you should concentrate the mind on the fingertips or on the stem of the brush. The brush is an extension of the arm, and the tip of the brush is the point of contact with the paper. Too much pressure breaks the back of the bristles, but too little pressure makes too thin a line. With the proper amount of pressure, the bristles fan out so that all of them come in contact with the paper. The bristles at the center of the brush, known as the *inochi-ge* or life-hair, are carefully selected for superior resiliency. With practice it is possible to feel the surface of the paper being gently etched by the *inochi-ge*, as if the bristles themselves were sensitive and alive. With an alert ear, you can even hear the sound of the brush on paper. This is an exhilarating sensation, and the longer that you can maintain it, the better will be the quality of your work. This is known as painting with the *hara* of the brush (Fig. 1-14). This is where you should concentrate your mind at first. In time your awareness will expand to take in other factors, such as the visual balance, relationship between strokes, and emotional qualities of the poem you are painting. Then you can begin to appreciate the state of enlightened awareness of past masters of the brush, that which takes in the whole, without stopping at the part.

Fig. 1-14

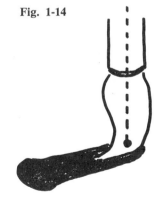

The Hand Is Quicker than the Eye

Increasingly in the modern world, old things are set aside for the sake of convenience or efficiency. The brush is hardly an efficient writing instrument. It is much harder to use than stiff and hard-tipped writing instruments like the ballpoint pen, or electronic word processing equipment. The brush was once the primary writing instrument of daily life in Japan, and most people assume that it has simply evolved into forms more suitable for the demands of modern life. It is neither desirable nor practical to go back to using the brush in daily life. But we should consider how it might be useful in developing certain endangered sensibilities. For all human faculties, whether brain, nerve, or muscle, lack of use leads to lack of function.

The atrophication of human sensibilities was something that Aldous Huxley warned of in his novel, *Brave New World*. The story's poetic hero of humanity, Helmholtz Watson, felt as if he had something important to say, and the power to say it, but lacked the means to do so: "If there was only some different way of writing . . . or something else to write about." Huxley criticized the loss of individuality in a world drugged with servitude and pleasure. This futuristic world was characterized by convenience, and lack of effort. People did not need to use their hands, because everything was done for them. What happens when people stop using their hands and rely on machines and laborsaving devices to do the majority of daily tasks? Huxley's warning to us all: use it or lose it. People often do not realize how far the deterioration has gone until they attempt to concentrate using the hands for an artistic or creative task.

Fig. 1-15

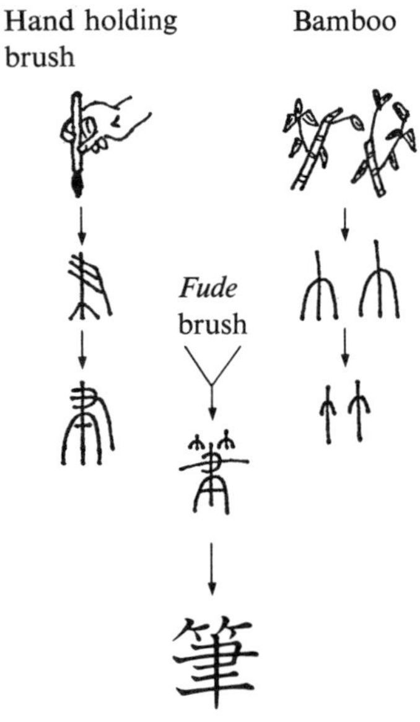

Hand holding brush   Bamboo

Fude brush

Dolphins are considered to be extremely intelligent, but they have never produced a culture. Biologists and anthropologists agree that it was the development of hands with opposable thumbs which enabled human beings to develop culture, while other creatures of high brain capacity did not. Without the hand, there would be no art, and no written language. The Japanese character for brush (*fude*) is a picture-symbol of a hand, holding a primitive brush (Fig. 1-15). Brain physiologists have clearly established that large areas of the brain are closely coordinated with eye and hand movements, far out of propotion with other parts of the body (Fig. 1-16). There is no doubt but that manual dexterity and eye-hand coordination promote brain development.

The Latin roots of the word *emancipation* suggest the act of (-tion) taking (-cip *capere*) out (e- *ex*) the hand (-man *manu*). To emancipate meant to

Fig. 1-16

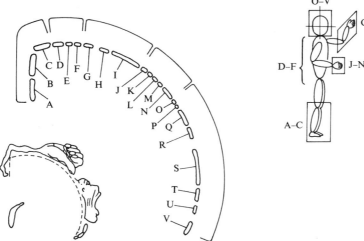

free the hands, presumably from manual labor, or shackles. Other English words deriving from the Latin root for hand include: manual, manacles, manicure, manufacture, manifest, maneuver, manuscript, manipulate, and legerdemain. The Japanese language too, recognizes a wide variety of associations for the word hand (*te/shu*), including the following: help (*hitode*), a means or way (*shudan*), trick or technique (*sono te*), skilled performance (*ude ga agaru*), trouble (*tesû*), involvement (*te o dasu*), turn or move (*teban*), and allowance (*te-ate*). Modern conveniences have emancipated the Japanese from many of the tasks and burdens which were once a routine part of daily life. Technology needs no advocate in Japan.

But many of the younger generation in Japan have stopped doing the things which traditionally maintained a high degree of manual dexterity. It was a highly dexterous people who invented the arts of paper folding, nail-less carpentry, world-class cutlery, and delicate scripts for brush writing. What about the coming generations?

Children in Japan play baseball, dodgeball, or hide-and-seek like children anywhere else. Western sports are so much a part of the school curriculum, that they are not considered foreign at all. Many children's toys today are electronic, and video games are extremely popular. Traditional toys, which depended on manual skill and imagination, are fast giving way to toys that are easier to use, and more flashy. Unlike the children of previous generations, many modern Japanese children cannot properly use chopsticks. Parents and teachers are often surprised to find that school children cannot tie their shoes by themselves, button jackets, fold cloth, or even peel an orange without help. It is easier to ask than to do. At a typical suburban elementary school in Osaka, a psychologist discovered that one-third of the children typically drew human figures without any fingers. Clearly, fingers were not something that played a central part in their own body awareness.

Unless manual skills are better reinforced at home and in the schools, Japan's famous work ethic may suffer in the next ten or twenty years. Indeed, it already has.

This problem is not limited to children. Atsuhiko Satô, of the Gakushû Jimu Nôritsu Research Center, which studies productivity and learning efficiency for office workers, conducted an eight-year study as long ago as the 1960s, to determine trends in the decline in skill in using chopsticks among Japanese adults. Over 5,000 Japanese men and women were tested during this period. Participants were asked to use chopsticks to transfer 200 soybeans, one at a time, from one dish to another, working against the clock. Some completed the task in 250 seconds or less, but the slow ones took 280 seconds or more. Only 55 percent of the people held the chopsticks correctly, and over 50 different styles of holding the chopsticks were noted among the remaining 45 percent. The slowest group was characterized by a large number of people in their twenties, but even housewives in their thirties were found to be surprisingly unskilled at using chopsticks. Incorrect use of chopsticks also correlated well with poor handwriting. A number of studies have been sponsored since then by corporations and universities, and reported in newspapers like the *Japan Economic Journal*, which indicate that the problem has only gotten worse.

Although Shodo today is practiced as a hobby or as an art form, in the past, all literate people used a brush. Calligraphy was the only form of writing, and was used for a vast range of formal and informal purposes. Many of the masterpieces which we have inherited from the past were simply the tidings of daily correspondence, not art for art's sake. Even common shop entrances and municipal ordinances were often brushed out with superb skill. Just as many of the classical masterpieces of music in the West once served Church, ceremonial, or social purposes, so calligraphy once served the functions of daily life in Japan. Perhaps the time has come for Japan to rediscover its own cultural heritage, and to share the best of it with the rest of the world.

The brush may not have the immediate practical use in daily life that it once did, but it is a marvelous tool for integrating mind and body, regardless of your cultural background. In the pursuit of progress and efficiency, we sometimes overlook the adverse side of new things. Conveniences make life easier, but they do not free us from its essential issues. When we stop using our hands, we risk the danger of becoming spectators of life, rather than participants in it. If we sit back and watch life go by, we may soon find that the hand is no longer quicker than the eye.

Principles for Controlling the Brush

The brush is an extension of the self. What we put on paper is a visible manifestation of what we are inside. By learning to control the brush we can produce better calligraphy, but through the brush we also gain better self-control. When mind and body are divided, life easily becomes twisted, out of joint. By coordinating mind, body, and brush, we can learn to calm and focus the mind on the task at hand.

Without concentration there is no control, and without control there is not sufficient energy to create. The principles then, for controlling the brush are:

1. **Weight forward, Elbow down.**
2. **Bend Elbow, Not Wrist.**
3. **Stem Vertical, Fingertips down.**
4. **Bristles Parallel.**
5. **Continuous Exhalation.**

Chapter 2

The Brush as an Instrument of Power

The Nature of Talent

The cormorant bird is used by fishermen in Japan to catch fish. It has a quick eye
and a ready strike, but it is not allowed to swallow its catch. Fishermen attach
a tight ring around its throat, and let the birds catch fish for them. Nature's choice
resources are often the first to be taken because they are so readily seen. In the
same way, the finest trees are often the first to be taken for lumber. Even preco-
cious children may find their talents quickly spoken for, only to end up in a gilded
cage of another's making.

Thus in the Oriental view, the early appearance of talent is not an auspicious
sign. It is the hawk, not the cormorant bird which represents the true nature of
talent. The hawk conceals its talons until the moment they are needed, and is
ready to use them any time. Falconry is a sport that was cultivated by the elite
members of the *samurai* warrior class. In it they found an ingenious example for
their own use of the sword. A sword must be kept in its sheath most of the time
if it is to remain serviceable for use.

Energy to the Japanese is found in the intensity of restraint, not in the reckless
frenzy of release. Often the person really in power is the general in the tent, silent,
calm, even taciturn. We see this in the reserved mask of the *Noh* Drama, and in
the imperturbable face of the martial artist. This sense of reserve is misleading, for
it conceals a spirited power within. When this force is brought to the fore, it is
often fleet as lightning. In this way Japanese organizations are often very hard to
read, and may take aggravatingly long to make a decision, but once it is made,
people are mobilized very quickly.

The Chinese sometimes compare the feeling of holding the brush to a dragon's
claw. But dragons are always portrayed with their talons fully extended, and if
the comparison is overdone in calligraphy, the arm becomes too tense. The point
in Shodo is not to be ever tense for action. The power that the artist unleashes in
the strokes springs from a state of reserve, or potential energy. Beginners often
become fatigued after a short period of calligraphy practice because they have not
yet learned how to use this latent strength. They expend too much energy when it
is not needed, and not enough when it is. Poor timing results in poor quality work.
Latent talent is more useful than talent which is always on display, particularly in
a crisis. Outside of the classroom, intelligence is measured not by what you already
know, but by how you perform when you do not know the answer in advance. The

sensitivity of the brush is a constant reminder that we must be fully relaxed and attentive in order to cope with the task at hand. Properly used, the brush helps cultivate a free and adaptable state of mind.

Keep the Centerline of the Brush in Contact with the Surface of the Paper

We have seen how the proper control of the brush brings the tip of every hair into contact with the paper, and how the *inochi-ge* at the center of the brush are among the longest and most resilient of the bristles. It is these bristles in particular which must remain in contact with the paper, and that contact is palpable with high quality handmade paper. Most people are accustomed to machine-made paper, which is smooth to the touch, and firm enough to provide the resistance needed for a hard-tipped writing utensil. But the brush is soft-tipped. The stem is usually hollow and made of wood, which makes it a good conductor for the delicate vibrations of the brush etching the surface of the paper.

Good paper gives the brush a slight resistance, just as ice resists a skate. How do you recognize handmade paper? If you hold it up to the light, you can see the thin lines of the surface on which it was made, and even some slight irregularities in the surface. Machine-made paper is more likely to be of an even consistency, less permeable to light. The cheaper kinds of paper are manufactured to be smooth on one side and rough on the other. It is best to avoid using this kind of paper, but if you must, the rough side is more likely to give you the resistance that you need. Resistance to the roughened surface produces the delicate sound of the brush on paper, and tells you that you are in touch.

While holding the brush properly, the best way to keep the center line in contact with the paper is to feel whether the hairs are actually etching the surface continuously, or occasionally skipping across it. When the brush is used correctly the tips of the hairs run parallel to the stroke, in the wake of the line. The brush may lean forward or back slightly in the direction of the stroke. But if the brush is held at an angle pointing away from the stroke, then the tips of the hairs also point off at an angle to the line. This causes only a small number of the hairs of the brush to actually be involved in painting the stroke (Fig. 2-1). Like a whip, the impact of the bristles is strongest at the tip. The greater the number of bristle tips

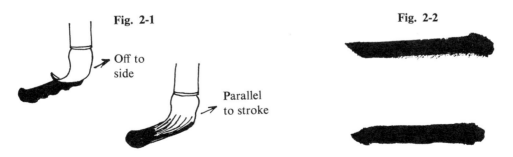

Fig. 2-1

Off to side

Parallel to stroke

Fig. 2-2

which strike the surface, the stronger the line appears. When a stroke is drawn with all of the hairs of the brush it has an elastic quality, like a cord under tension. If the stroke is drawn using only a part of the brush it looks slack, like a string being dragged along a rough surface (Fig. 2-2).

Use the Fingertips of the Free Hand to Support the Paper

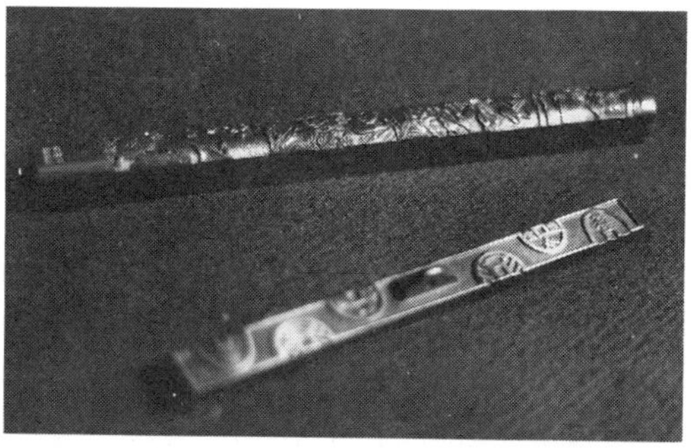

Because wet paper tends to adhere to both the brush and the writing surface, it is necessary to support it with paper weights from above, and a water-repellent cloth from below. The cloth prevents the ink from running or marking the surface under the paper, and the weights keep it from sticking to the brush. Using a paper weight (*bunchin*, Fig. 2-3) provides stability, but it has several disadvan-

Fig. 2-3

tages. First, it covers the top portion of the paper. Like an unwanted curtain, it conceals part of the stage. You can move it around as you go, but that is distracting. If you leave it in place, it throws the work off balance, by leaving too large a space at the top of the page.

The second disadvantage is that it makes your free hand lazy. Chinese characters (*kanji*) were designed to be written with the brush held in the right hand. The left hand is then free to support the paper against the movement of the brush. This is not as much of a handicap as it might seem to left-handers, because the whole arm is engaged in the movement, not just the hand. Furthermore, the task is so new and unfamiliar that right-handers seem to enjoy no particular advantage in

Fig. 2-4

the beginning. Letting the left hand lay idle reinforces the bad habit of painting with the wrist rather than the whole arm. Even if you do use a paper weight, as you must when the paper is too large to control the edges, the free hand should be used as and where needed, to support the paper against the motion of the brush. In this way the paper is always held taut, and the left hand maintains a constant awareness of what the right hand is doing (Fig. 2-4).

Strokes drawn from top to bottom are supported at the top of the paper. Strokes drawn from left to right are supported at the left. In principle, the anchor is needed above or before the origin of the stroke; although in practice, small movements of the fingertips or forearm usually provide adequate support. The free hand is not as busy as it might appear. Painting with both hands gives you greater awareness and control, just like driving a car with manual transmission keeps you more attuned to the road.

Begin the Stroke Clearly, Accelerate without Hesitation, Come to a Clean Stop

Precisely speaking, there are no truly simple lines in calligraphy. A single stroke, such as the character for the number one (*ichi*), has a distinct beginning, middle, and end, creating a definite articulation at both ends (Fig. 2-5). Even a small dot painted with the brush should contain all three stages, though they may be quite subtle. Articulating the stroke in three stages (*ki-hitsu, sô-hitsu, shû-hitsu*) helps you execute it with purpose from beginning to end. Otherwise the length of the stroke takes precedence, and the beginning or ending lack articulation. Wherever the calligrapher's concentration is momentarily broken the stroke appears hesitant or feeble.

Nevertheless, the sense of articulation can be overdone. Many basic strokes in calligraphy are not actually straight lines, but start and end with a slight articulation. Beginners usually try to produce the accented shape at the end of the stroke by slowly drawing an outline of that shape with the brush. This does produce a likeness in form, but articulating the stroke in this way forces the brush to move at a single speed from beginning to end, with no sense of acceleration or rhythm. The proper way to articulate the end of the stroke is by accelerating to a clean stop, not by drawing the shape. The acceleration of the brush causes a gradual thickening of the line while the rapid stop causes the bristles to fan out and create a sudden thickening of the stroke.

The effect is similar to that of a skier coming out of a long descent to a hairpin stop, causing the snow to pile up suddenly. The sudden suspension of movement does not throw the skier off balance, but enables him to strike off in a new direction, with full control and balance. The brush operates in the same way, bending like a spring under compression at the end of the stroke, but once it leaves the paper, all of the hairs remain parallel (Fig. 2-6). This allows you to keep going with little or no need for adjustment. Drawing the outline of the stroke's features

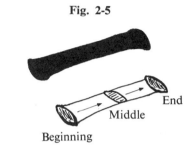

Fig. 2-5

End
Middle
Beginning

Fig. 2-6

is like walking, rather than skiing the course. The slow speed and poor rhythm of the brush causes the bristles to become limp and twisted, making it difficult to continue painting without readjusting the brush.

Because the hand is quicker than the eye, it is easy to feel like you are getting ahead of yourself. Rapid movements threaten to upset balance. It may be a natural reflex to resist the movement with tension, but that is exactly the wrong thing to do. Tensing up causes a skier to fall. In calligraphy it causes you to overshoot, or to exaggerate the strokes, resulting in distorted proportions or insufficient space to finish the character. All beginners feel awkward at first, and losing your balance is not much fun. But balance comes easily once you get the knack through practice.

At first, it may seem easier to paint everything at the same speed, but this habit can handicap you in the long run. Like a bicycle, the brush can only maintain its precarious upright position if it is in motion. Small children practice with training wheels, which give an artificial sense of stability. In the same way, resting the forearm on your free wrist or on the edge of the table gives an added feeling of stability, but it prevents you from moving the arm freely at the proper speed. Think of the strokes in terms of speed not shape, and you will advance much more quickly in your practice. Your calligraphy will have greater visual impact if you start each stroke slowly, speed up and bring the brush to a clean stop. Looking at a masterpiece of calligraphy, you can recognize this effect even many centuries after it was created.

Strike the Surface of the Paper with Every Hair of the Brush

Fig. 2-7

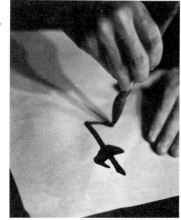

Strictly speaking, the brush actually accelerates to a pause rather than to a dead stop. This allows it to change direction and move into the next stroke without losing momentum. The pause merely suspends motion, without stopping it. To do this, the brush must be raised slightly at the end of a stroke. As the brush draws up, the hairs taper to a point, and may flip over to lay a different face of the brush on the paper for the next stroke (Fig. 2-7). This happens whether or not the brush leaves the surface of the paper. Painting on all sides of the brush automatically corrects and realigns the bristles as you go. It also extends the usable life of the brush.

Lifting the brush is the only way to paint with all of the bristles without bending the wrist or tilting the stem. Moving the brush up and down in three dimensions makes full use of the resilient properties of the hair of the brush. It also helps you keep the centerline of the *inochi-ge* in contact with the paper. Each principle for use of the brush works in concert with the others. If you do one well, you are likely to do the others automatically. If you lose one, you are likely to lose them all. The concept is not difficult to understand, but it takes practice to be able to do it consistently. Learn to paint with every hair of the brush, and it will become a living extension of your arm.

Keep the Flow of Energy between the Strokes on and off the Paper

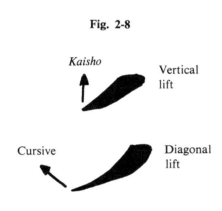

Fig. 2-8

Kaisho

Vertical lift

Cursive

Diagonal lift

We will consider the difference between formal and informal script styles in a later chapter, but it is worth noting here that different styles use different stroke endings, which are produced by a different use of the brush. In theory, formal stroke endings are produced by lifting the brush vertically from the page, clearly accenting the end of the stroke. For informal stroke endings the brush is lifted on a diagonal, as a continuation of the stroke (Fig. 2-8). It is unusual however, to find a style which is all one or the other. Like the clothing that we wear, there are many degrees of formality.

The formal style of writing is characterized by articulation. Each stroke is written separately. The brush is lifted off of the paper at the end of the stroke, almost at right angles to the page. It is permissible to adjust the brush between strokes as needed, though preferably not in the middle of a character. Formal scripts build each character architecturally, stroke by stroke.

The more abbreviated cursive styles of writing are characterized by fluidity. The brush is lifted off of the paper on a diagonal line, as an extension of the stroke itself. The strokes are intertwined rather than assembled. To adjust the brush between strokes in the cursive style would break the *Ki-myaku*, or flow of Ki energy which connects all of the strokes, both on and off of the paper. In cursive calligraphy, the adjustment of the brush is made at the end of a phrase or character, or when the brush is refilled with ink.

It may seem to be a near impossible task to gauge the many factors of pressure, ink, speed and form. Experience is the best guide, but there is one little known shortcut, and that is to fully saturate the brush with ink. If you only apply ink to the tip of the brush, you will find that the bristles become tangled and twisted very easily. If you fill a straw with water, you can keep the water from leaking out as long as you keep your fingertip tightly over the upper end of the straw. As soon as air is allowed to enter at the top, the water pours out. If the tip is sealed at one end, the only way to get the water out is to suck on the straw at the open end. Since no air can enter from either side, the straw flattens under the pressure. This is what happens when you paint with a fully saturated brush. As the ink is drawn out by the absorbent paper, the brush binds from within and becomes very firm. This gives the hairs of the brush a flexible spine. Like the ankle support of a good ski boot, it allows the brush to make turns without spraining or twisting, and keeps the hairs relatively parallel. If air is allowed to enter at the top, the spine breaks like a pack of loose straw.

Preserving the Cutting Edge

In Chinese lore, there is a story of a blade which cut very well, but did not wear. The large cleaver used in Oriental cooking is named after an Imperial Chinese cook, who lived during the period of the Civil Wars, around two or three hundred B.C. The Prince noted that his cook had an exceptional ability to cleave meat from the bone without damaging or dulling the blade. His movements were intriguing: clean, rhythmic, and uninhibited. The cook explained that the secret of his craft lay in the search for the Tao (dô), or way. When the beginner cuts meat, he looks at the side of beef, and hacks his way through it by sight, wearing out a new blade every month. After three years, he learns to feel his way by hand, and need not look at the structure of bone and muscle. After long years, if he masters his trade, the meat yields to the blade without resistance. He no longer looks at the meat, but finds his way effortlessly in the natural harmony of the Way. In this way the cook had used the same knife for 19 years, though its blade was as sharp and smooth as new. Even allowing for the Chinese love of exaggeration, there is no doubt that superior skill preserves the life of any instrument, the brush included.

Many Oriental stories suggest the importance of sensing intuitively, rather than relying on sight alone. Stories of blind master swordsmen can only be interpreted in this way. The eye is not as good a judge of proportion and balance as we would like to think, as any beginning driver can tell you. The eye is easily fooled by optical illusions. Magic tricks depend for their effectiveness on the fact that the hand is often quicker than the eye. The sense of balance depends to a greater degree on visceral or internal factors than on visual cues, or at least it should. In one experiment, people were asked to try to keep their balance while standing on a motionless floor, as the walls moved around them. The revolving walls were decorated in bright vertical stripes. Experienced Judo players stood calmly, while people lacking this kind of training were confused by the movement of the whirling stripes, and became dizzy and unsure. There was no physical reason for anyone to lose balance, but those untrained in the martial arts did. Unless you have a calm center based on an intuitive perception of space, you are likely to lose your balance or concentration in a complicated task. The mind which is rough is likely to abuse any instrument or person that gets in its way. The best way to preserve the cutting edge is to preserve the calm center.

One of the most renowned swordsmen in Japanese history, Yagyû Tajima no Kami Munenori, was also a student of Zen. His teacher, Takuan Sôhô, wrote a letter to him on the relationship between Zen and swordsmanship, which again related the cutting edge to the concept of vision. Takuan said that in looking at a tree, if the mind stops at a single leaf, it loses sight of the whole tree. However, if the mind is open in looking at the tree, it takes in all of the leaves at once. Concentrating on an opponent's weapon, you will see nothing else. Enlarge your field of vision to take in the whole, and you will not be trapped by the part. Gain insight into the essence, rather than merely looking at the surface.

The lore of the Japanese sword is a connoisseur's collection of the cutting edge. But a distinction is made between the sword which gives life (*katsujin-ken*), and the sword which takes it away (*satsujin-ken*). A sword tempered by a mentally unstable swordsmith may have been sharp, but it was also rumored to lead its owner into death. If the character of the swordsmith was humane, this too would be reflected in the weapon, which would protect the owner as well as others from harm. Representing the two extremes were the terrible Muramasa, and the chivalrous Masamune swords. Both swords had exceptionally fine cutting edges. Placed upright against the current of a stream, the Muramasa blade would sever any leaf which touched it, while the leaves seemed to avoid the blade of the Masamune. The story may be apocryphal, but the lesson is clear. The sword of death is raw and exposed; the sword of life remains in its sheath, but it also remains a sword.

The brush is treated with the same respect. The teacher (*Sensei*) rarely lends a favorite brush to a student. It is considered a special privilege to be able to use the *Sensei's* brush. A brush which has been properly trained writes exceptionally well, even better than a new brush, and far more responsive than one which has been abused by the beginner's hand. A well-trained brush may last for years, while a novice can ruin a brush in a few short months. Superior skill preserves the cutting edge.

Training Freehand

Human beings seem driven to improve their lot through technology, through improved efficiency or laborsaving devices. Even cultures which have only recently been exposed to modern technology are highly vulnerable to devices which make life easier. Yet making something easier does not always make it better. If things are made too easy, we may be freed from the burden of work, but robbed of the opportunity for self-development. This trade-off is also evident with shortcuts in the learning process, particularly in the arts.

Anyone can project the voice using electronic amplification. It takes an accomplished actor to be heard at a whisper even at the back of the auditorium. You do not gain this ability by practicing with a public address system. It takes a beginner several months to learn to produce the first sound on the Japanese *shakuhachi*, or bamboo flute, much less produce anything which sounds like music. Yet there is now available a mouthpiece adapter which allows you to produce a sound on the first try. This may be a way to encourage impatient people to start, but it is unlikely to help develop the proper breath control or concentration to play the instrument well. Training aids may be all right for children, but they should not be confused with the real thing. A child uses training wheels in the brief transition between tricycle and bicycle, but this is a temporary crutch, not a destination in itself.

Knowing this, the serious calligrapher is not inclined to rely on training aids, although many are available. Paper weights hold the paper down for you. Special paper allows you to trace on top of the faint image of pre-printed characters for practice. Felt undercloth is available which is ruled and sectioned, to help you keep your characters in straight columns. Preground ink is available which saves you the trouble of grinding the ink yourself. There are even refillable cartridge brush-pens, tipped with plastic fibers or rubber sponge, which give the impression of brush strokes, but with the fingertip control of a hard-tipped pen. And you can even do crude calligraphy on a computer. But none of these give you the benefits of the freehand brush on handmade paper. Some things get worse with improvement.

Principles for Expressing Energy on Paper

Nothing begins well without motivation, the desire of the mind to extend beyond itself and reach a goal. But as long as the incentives are external we tend to be caught in a cycle of stimulus and response. When the locus of control is outside of ourselves we are forced to follow rather than lead. Initiative is a mental habit. It cannot be faked when it is lacking to begin with. In order to take the lead in life we need to be tremendously resourceful, and always strive to cultivate our latent potential. Through the medium of the brush, Shodo can help you develop the ability to gather and release energy, which is the real secret of initiative. The principles for releasing this energy are:

1. **Contact the Paper Surface.**
2. **Use the Free Hand for Support.**
3. **Accelerate to a Clean Stop.**
4. **Use Every Hair of the Brush.**
5. **Maintain Energy on and off the Paper.**

Chapter 3

Space Dynamics and Dimensionality

Seeing Is Selective

Two people can look at the same thing, but what they see depends a great deal on attention and interest. Not everyone focuses on the same features when they look at another person. One is drawn to clothing, another to facial expressions, another to hairstyle (Fig. 3-1). Visual information comes to us as a whole, rather than in linear sequence. But we select optical priorities by the way that we organize this mass of visual data. The eye wanders freely across a photograph, seeing selectively rather than taking in the whole. No two people scan a photograph in the same way (Fig. 3-2). The pattern of eye movement depends on the purpose of the observer and on the visual interest of the subject. Seeing straight is only a figure of speech.

Printed text is linear, but surprisingly reading is not. Of course the eyes follow the rough sequence of the text, but careful measures with an eye scanning device show that eye movements in reading are anything but straight. Depending on reading speed and level of interest, eye motion tends to be characterized by frequent fixations and looplike oval movements which overlap considerably, and may take

Fig. 3-1

Fig. 3-2

48

Fig. 3-3

in several lines of text at once. Speed readers can scan a page in a diagonal sweep, and still maintain a high degree of comprehension. No matter how complex Japanese characters may appear to the Western eye, native speakers can read and skim them without any apparent handicap. Japanese children often learn to recognize relatively complex picto-graphic characters before they learn to read the far simpler, but abstract phonetic symbols.

In principle, learning to read Japanese *kanji* is no different than learning to recognize constellations in the night sky. The strokes are formed into recognizable picture elements, which are readily combined to form more complex characters. One difference between a picture and a picto-graphic character is the degree of closure in the drawing. Psychologists use closure in picture recognition as one measure of intelligence. The subject is shown a series of drawings. The first several have only a few traces of lines. Subsequent pictures are gradually filled in to suggest, and then plainly reveal a drawing of a familiar object. The task is to identify the picture as soon as you can guess what it is (Fig. 3-3). A quick mind recognizes the picture before it becomes apparent, while a slow one may not be able to identify it until it is obvious.

The eyes are an organ of the brain, and their movement reflects its activity. Shodo involves more than looking, it requires accurately reproducing what you see. By giving depth to the flat surface of the page, you are revealing superior powers of perception. Children draw without perspective. As they mature they learn to see and express things with more of the depth, movement, and subtlety of the real world. But the fact that many adults are incapable of drawing beyond a child's level suggests that their perceptual powers are still underdeveloped. Seeing may be selective, but it is also subtle, as any attempt to draw from nature will quickly show. A good drawing is an art of omission, reducing the picture to its essential lines. Calligraphy is an art of articulation, bringing the character into sharp relief in all its subtle grandeur. Once you learn to control the brush and express energy on the paper, the next step is to give dimension to the flat surface.

Saturate the Brush, and Feather off the Excess Ink

We have seen how the brush must be saturated with ink in order to help stabilize the spine of the brush, and to provide an ink reservoir capable of painting a series of characters. But to saturate does not mean to drench. The brush should not drip, for any leaks onto the paper almost automatically disqualify the work. On the other hand, if you apply too much pressure on the side of the ink dish to remove

Fig. 3-4

the excess ink, you may break the ink reservoir, and end up with too little ink to complete the first character. The solution is to feather off the excess ink from the outer bristles, by lightly running the brush against the edge of the ink dish. The raised portion (*oka*) in the center of special calligraphy ink dishes is for this purpose (Fig. 3-4).

You need apply no more pressure than the weight of the brush itself, for this is enough to remove the dripping ink, without breaking into the supply of ink held by the bristles at the center of the brush. Even so, the way that you apply the brush to the paper in the initial stroke may break the seal of the reserve and cause too much ink to leak out. This produces a blotting effect called *nijimi* (Fig. 3-5).

Sometimes this is a desirable effect, as long as it does not blot in the white space between adjacent strokes. With high quality paper, finely ground ink, and a skilled use of the brush, this effect can be quite beautiful, causing the ink to fan out in fine hair thin rays like a halo around the stroke. *Nijimi* strokes should occur at the beginning of a phrase, and should not be repeated at mechanical intervals.

The beauty of a wet stroke is often heightened by the gradual transition of the characters in the column into dry, airy strokes called *kasure* (Fig. 3-6). With a drier brush, the ink can be fanned out so lightly that it brings the texture of the paper into sharp relief. Because the transition is gradual, it is best to plan the application of ink to the brush so that the wet strokes in one column are not immediately adjacent to the *nijimi* strokes in the next column. It is very difficult to apply just the right amount of ink so that the brush runs dry at the right moment. If this happens, you can refresh the brush by briefly dipping the tip in the ink, without fully saturating it again.

Fig. 3-5   **Fig. 3-6**

The extremes of *nijimi* and *kasure* are both difficult to produce. A stroke which is charged with too much ink may blot into the adjacent strokes and make the character illegible. A stroke which is too dry may run out of ink or skip in places, making it too weak to carry the energy to the next stroke. The placement of wet

50

and dry strokes is a matter of the original artist's composition. In attempting to copy the work, recreating the strokes is a question of interpretation and artistic skill. Learning to recognize and appreciate the position of *nijimi* and *kasure* strokes is a matter of cultivated taste. Like the flowers in a Japanese flower arrangement, similar elements are almost never placed adjacently at the same height.

Fig. 3-7

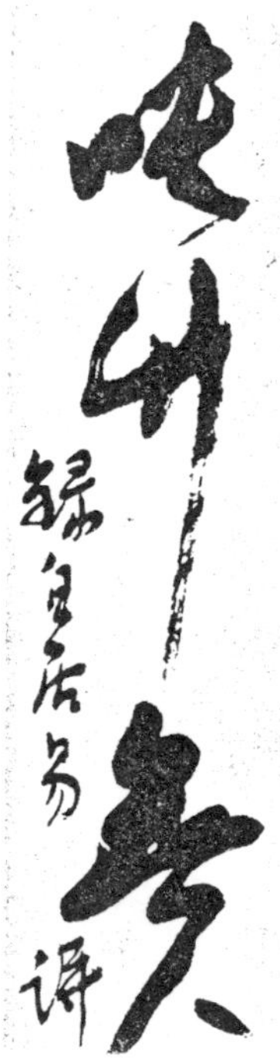

Fig. 3-8

Dark, wet, blotting strokes correspond to the bass notes on a musical scale, while the light, dry, airy strokes are like high-pitched soprano notes. A good piece of music artfully blends the two, but only seldom goes to the extremes at either end of the scale. By adjusting the tone of the ink, you can create height and depth in the visual scale. When combined with variation in the size of each character, you can create a feeling of movement in the visual field (Fig. 3-7). *Nijimi* and *kasure* are usually only considered appropriate for cursive or semi-cursive scripts, while the more formal printed styles contain mostly standard black strokes in the middle range (Fig. 3-8). After learning the control and discipline of the standard strokes, you can venture to the extremes without losing your balance.

Apply Minimal Pressure for Maximal Effect

Ink is produced by grinding an inkstick (*sumi*) on a hand carved and polished slate grinding stone called a *suzuri*. This stone functions like a whetstone, which sharpens and refines the blade of a knife. The inkstick should be held vertically, and rubbed gently in a small amount of water on the surface, in a circular motion (Fig. 3-9). Like the brush, the *sumi* is held vertically. Holding the stick perpendicular to the stone keeps the bottom of the inkstick flat and even. Very little pressure is needed to release particles of ink from their glued matrix. To emphasize this point, *sumi* was said to be best ground by a small child or a young nurse. Putting too much muscle into the process may dam-

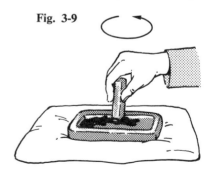

Fig. 3-9

age the inkstick, and is more likely to break off undissolved chunks than to liberate small particles of carbon. Grinding with too much tension can also cramp the free motion of your arm, which is poor preparation for brush writing.

Whether you grind your own ink or use preground liquid ink (*boku-jû*), you will still get an optimal effect by painting with minimal pressure. The point is not to bear down on the brush, but rather to open and close the fan of bristles at the tip, without breaking open the reservoir of ink stored in the bristles above it.

People have a tendency to physically press down on things when they concentrate. However this interferes with the ability to relax, and makes it difficult to move nimbly. It is better to move like a cat, staying alert, but without getting so dug in to what you are doing that you lose adroitness. Physical bearing affects mental attitude. Over concentration can leave you tense and tired. Calligraphy is spirited, not solemn.

Fig. 3-10   **Fig. 3-11**

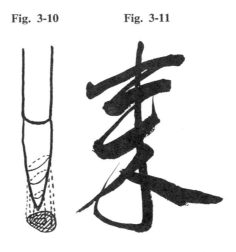

The brush is buoyant because it rises and falls on the surface. The traces that it leaves on the paper are two-dimensional, but the brush itself moves freely up and down (Fig. 3-10). This vertical movement creates variations in the thickness of the line. The contrast of thick and thin lines crossing at various angles gives the piece a three-dimensional quality (Fig. 3-11).

Speed up on the Straight Strokes, Slow down on the Curves

Fig. 3-12

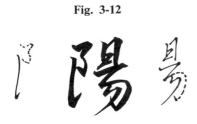

We have already compared balance of a brush to that of a bicycle, and how its handles changes in direction in much the same way. Unless you move the brush at an appropriate speed for the line, you are likely to lose balance or veer off course. This speed is partly determined by the amount of ink in the brush. To give the proper amount of tone to the stroke, a wet brush is moved more quickly and a dry brush more slowly. In general a straight line should be fast and a curved line slow (Fig. 3-12).

As long as the brush is in contact with the paper, it will discharge ink. It must be kept in constant motion, except for a pause to change direction or a sharp turn. Usually the brush will be almost off of the page at this moment, delicately poised on the tip before taking off on a new angle. This is often necessary for

Fig. 3-13

complicated cursive script where you can easily get confused in the tangle if you do not pause and take it in sections (Fig. 3-13).

It is impossible to guess the exact speed of the brush with which the original piece was written. It is also impossible to duplicate the original brush, amount of ink, and consistency of the paper. However, you must come reasonably close, within fairly wide limits, or you will be unable to make a good copy. A work of calligraphy is actually produced in four dimensions, not three, because the speed and timing of the brush is as important as its height or lateral movement. The traces of this dynamic movement of the brush are only visible on paper in two dimensions.

Look at both the Figure and the Ground

In calligraphy, spatial awareness means the ability to project space dynamics on paper. Space has both a positive and negative aspect, known as figure and ground. We tend to focus exclusively on the figure, and to ignore the ground, but in Shodo, both are equally important. The more subtle and refined the character, the more interesting the white space in between. Many ancient works of calligraphy have been lost or destroyed, but wood or stone-carved templates remain, from which rubbings are produced. Like the negative print of a photograph, these rubbings reverse figure and ground, but the principle is the same. In some ways, the white figure with a black ground actually makes the ground, or space between the strokes, easier to see. Note that the spaces enclosed by crossing lines sometimes have a distinct geometric identity (Fig. 3-14). If you ignore the spaces and only copy the lines, you may be able to produce a vague figure likeness, but the forgery will be obvious.

Fig. 3-14

The figure-ground relationship applies even when the character is too simple to have any crossed lines. O-gishi used the same simple character in one piece dozens of times, and never wrote it twice in the same way (Fig. 3-15). It takes tremendous creativity to say the same thing over twenty times without repeating yourself. Flowing water refreshes our senses because its simple sound is never exactly the same. Stagnant water offends the senses. Through habit or neglect, human beings be-

Fig. 3-15

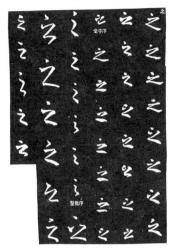

come stagnant when they stop growing. Art offers a remedy to a stagnant life, because it articulates and shapes our own renewal. Not only the paper, but we ourselves gain a new dimension when we paint and see in this way.

It is not only the inside of the character which forms the ground, but the external geometry as well. The difficulty that a student has in balancing the parts of a character comes from paying too little attention to its geometric profile. Like a human face, each character has a contour, which can be roughly fit into a circle, rectangle, triangle, or sometimes more complex outline (Fig. 3-16). These shapes are obvious when pointed out, but otherwise are often missed entirely because too much attention is given to the figure rather than

Fig. 3-16

Diagonal	Circular	Inverse triangle	Triangle	Horizon-tal	Vertical	Wide square	Tall square
万	米	可	土	一	月	口	国
毋	赤	寸	立	四	凡	北	度
夕	寺	丁	山	四	片	政	門

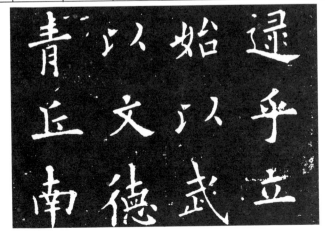

54

Fig. 3-17

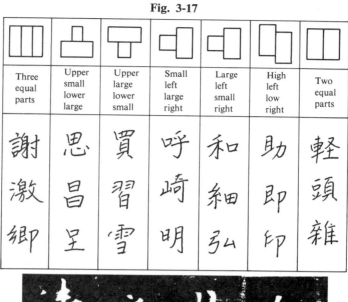

Three equal parts	Upper small lower large	Upper large lower small	Small left large right	Large left small right	High left low right	Two equal parts
謝 激 郷	思 昌 呈	買 習 雪	呼 崎 明	和 細 弘	助 即 印	軽 頭 雜

the ground. There are even profiles within profiles, which can be discovered by piecing the various subshapes together (Fig. 3-17). This exercise will sharpen your perception, and give your calligraphy more dimension.

Maintain the Proper Distance and Angle between Strokes

Michelangelo said that trifles make perfection. There could hardly be anything more minute than the subtle angles and proportions which spell the difference between excellent and mediocre calligraphy. When the student's work is completed, the *Sensei* corrects it by painting in corrections in red ink, on top of the student's

Fig. 3-18

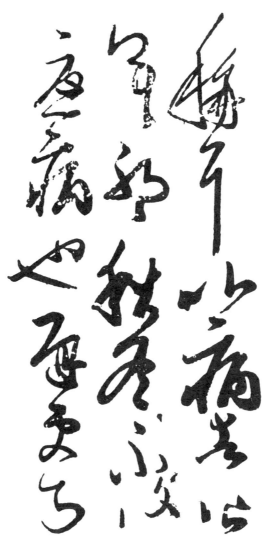

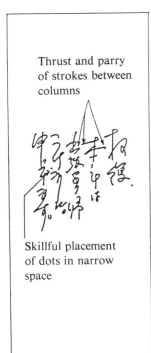

Thrust and parry
of strokes between
columns

Skillful placement
of dots in narrow
space

black strokes. Sometimes the difference is so slight that it seems almost arbitrary. However you should remember that the *Sensei* sees more, and takes more stroke relationships into account in making the correction.

There should be an interplay between strokes, even between characters in different columns. The thrust of one extended stroke is parried by the skillful dodge of another (Fig. 3-18). This is rarely a deliberate process at first, as there is too much else to be concerned with when you are absorbed in painting. But the greater the awareness of the person behind the brush, the more such factors come into account. The parallelism, perpendicularity, and alignment of strokes can play a subtle but crucial role in the overall impact of the piece.

Attention to these largely unconscious factors can also indicate things about a person's health, psychological balance, and intelligence. Handwriting analysis is still a young science in Japan, but brush calligraphy reveals a great deal about various dimensions of the human personality. By working with good models (*tehon*), and paying close attention to the position and relationship of strokes, we have an opportunity to improve and give structure to our own character.

Types of Seeing

Seeing is a form of intelligence, a way of organizing the bewildering array of data that impinges on our senses. We do not see everything that meets the eye. We tend to see what is useful to us. This is necessary for survival, and helps us avoid danger. When not pressed by immediate needs, we see by mental association. One thing reminds us of another, and sets off a chain of thought. This helps us to invent, communicate, and imagine new ways of doing things. When the mind is open, we see by discovery. That which was never before noticed suddenly becomes obvious. This kind of seeing leads to creative insight. The total operation of functional, associative, serendipitous, and intuitive seeing develops imagination, for which art is the supreme language.

Language is analytical, temporal, and linear. Art is Gestalt, presentational, and immediate. Language and art are both forms of thinking, and Shodo is both language and art. Containing elements of both, it helps us to think with both sides of the brain. The visual arts include architecture, sculpture, and painting. Works of visual art impress us as vividly existing in space, whether we walk inside, around, or in front of them. This sensation results from the positive use of negative space.

Painting makes use of implied lines, textures, and proportions to lead the eye in a somewhat predetermined path. Not everyone sees a work of art in the same way, but the artist has greater control over our perception than we realize. There are no absolutes in art. The beloved works of one age are often despised by the next, and genius often goes unrecognized in its own time. A well-educated person is able to transcend, or at least temporarily suspend the limited values of the present, and see the world vicariously through the eyes of another. This does not mean that anything goes. The classics have endured because people long since disposed of the rubbish, and made great efforts to keep the best. The ravages of time and politics take a toll, but much of the best endures.

But how can we as Westerners judge quality in an art like calligraphy, which was born in a foreign culture and a distant time? The traditional way of developing artistic taste is through exposure to the classics. Mass media, with its unprecedented barrage of commercial and political art, has considerably confused and lowered contemporary standards. In this situation, to ignore the classics is to commit artistic suicide. Shodo helps develop the skills of aesthetic vision through the basic elements of line, proportion, and space dynamics. Unlike modern art, however, it has one objective element: it must be legible. Certain standards and rules have developed over the centuries, and modern attempts to improve upon them have been largely unsuccessful.

The concept of space in Western art has undergone a number of radical changes, each of which has enriched the ones before. The flat vertical planes of medieval European painting gave way to the three dimensional perspective of the Renaissance. The Impressionists made space diffuse, the Cubists gave it dimension, and abstract painters made it almost irrelevant. Art enriches the whole idea of space. The thought that space could be other than what it appears is the product of a searching imagination. Hard-nosed realists may consider such pursuits to be a waste of time. However, many things that are now accepted as common sense were once ridiculed as dangerous nonsense or heresy. Galileo faced execution as a heretic for claiming that the earth was other than it appeared.

Spatial Intelligence

Intelligence was once considered a matter of mental brawn. In 1884 at the London Exhibition, Sir Francis Galton tried to prove that intelligence was a function of the size of the head. He measured the head size of several prominent British scientists, but their heads seemed no different from those of ordinary British citizens. Intelligence tests have become more sophisticated in the twentieth century, but most measures of intelligence are still limited to verbal and mathematical aptitude, or knowledge of a particular subject matter. Many tests today have come under attack for their cultural bias or questionable validity. Do the tests really measure the skills that will be needed outside of school? Do we need to broaden still further our concept of intelligence?

Linguistic, logical, and quantitative measures of intelligence are often misleading, because real life problem solving involves a greater range of abilities, including such intangibles as poise, physical coordination, spatial awareness, and interpersonal skills. For a balanced view of life, we need to learn to see with the eyes of the artist as well as the scientist.

Measures of spatial intelligence do exist, but their emphasis is heavily biased toward reasoning about visual forms. Typical paper tests ask the student to match complex forms which are similar in appearance, or to visualize how something would appear from a different angle (Fig. 3-19). These skills may be quite useful to

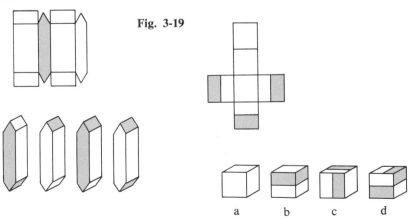

Fig. 3-19

a   b   c   d

Fig. 3-20

Thematic Apperception
Test (TAT)

Rorschach
Inkblot

geologists and engineers, but they depend far more on reasoning than imagination. Psychologists also use tests of visual thinking, notably the Rorschach Inkblot and Thematic Apperception Tests (Fig. 3-20). But in both of these cases it is verbal associations which are being measured, and not visual perception. The illustration serves simply as a visual stimulus for verbal thinking. Tests of creativity, which are still not widely accepted as valid, focus heavily on the use of reasoning to find alternative solutions to a problem (Fig. 3-21). Tests of three-dimensional visualization, verbal association, and creative problem solving each use visual thinking in some measure, but none of them focuses on the skill of seeing itself.

Fig. 3-21

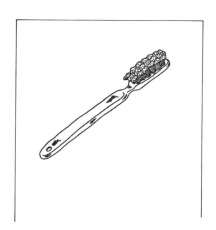

For example . . .

Scrub brush.

List alternate uses
for a toothbrush . . .

Plant label stick.

The branch of study which concentrated almost exclusively on the process of visual perception was Gestalt Psychology, originating in Germany in the early 1900s. Best known for its observation that the whole is greater than the sum of the parts, Gestalt Psychology contains a number of insights which are extremely helpful in understanding the art of calligraphy. We have already looked at the Gestalt concept of figure and ground. The figure is the part of the picture that we most easily notice. It requires a shift in perspective to see the background. It is possible to draw a picture in which the figure and ground are almost interchangeable, as in the famous example of

Fig. 3-22

vases and faces (Fig. 3-22). The eye can focus on one or the other in rapid sequence, but not both simultaneously.

Our brain organizes visual data in terms of perceptual groupings. As with figure and ground, groupings of lines and shapes can also undergo a shift of focus. Proximity dictates the initial grouping, but a slight alteration of the figure can cause us to group the lines in an entirely different way (Fig. 3-23). This is very important in Shodo, where the proximity of strokes is a critical element in legibility. The art of brush writing, as opposed to simple handwriting, is one of stretching the perceptual limits of a group of strokes, without rendering the character illegible. There is a great deal of leeway allowed, but somehow the spell can be broken if the process is carried too far. Taffy stretches just so far until it breaks. Just how far you can stretch the field of legibility is a matter of experience and artistic judgment (Fig. 3-24). The misplacement of a single stroke in this field can cause the whole thing to come undone. In order to recreate the spell with your own brush, you need to sustain the energy between strokes, and to grasp the relationship of the strokes as a whole.

Simplicity is another factor which determines perceptual groupings. The brain

Fig. 3-23

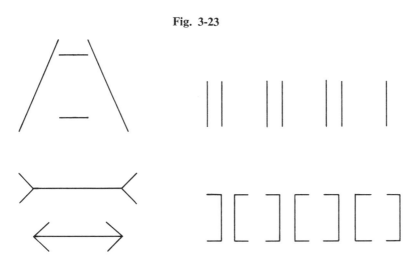

Fig. 3-24a   Fig. 3-24b   Fig. 3-24c

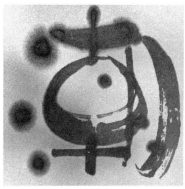

tends to construct and retain the concept of an object which is the most intelligible with the least effort. This takes place on various levels of sophistication, depending on the maturity of the person's perception. Small children mistake visual changes for physical changes, believing that objects actually get smaller as they get farther away, or that the moon is actually following them when they ride down the highway. It requires some perceptual skill to read a picture, which is why children often have difficulty building a simple model from illustrated instructions. Primitive peoples have been known to have difficulty recognizing their own family members in a photograph. An anthropologist named Colin Turnbill described in his book, *The Forest People*, how a Pygmy boy of fifteen who had left the forest for the first time in his life, had trouble believing that large animals at a great distance were other than insects. The ability to track and recognize an object despite perceptual changes is something we take for granted, but it is a learned skill.

The ability to reduce complex visual data to a simple concept is very useful. But ironically, it is this very ability to form and conserve concepts which sometimes blinds us to the pure act of seeing itself. The artist sees the familiar in an unfamiliar light, and thereby creates forms that we never before imagined. By sticking to a familiar way of looking at things, we tend to form stereotypes, and ignore visual relationships that have no apparent utility. The artist helps us experience a new way of looking at something by giving it a vivid visual description. But if the expression is too subjective it becomes unintelligible. Everyone has experienced the random musings of the stream of consciousness, but unedited writing is rarely worth reading.

There is a fine line between genius and madness. The artist's challenge is to skirt this line, but remain on the proper side. Most art forms have safeguards, in the form of traditions and conventions, and Shodo is no exception. Calligraphy is painted writing, and therefore must be legible to qualify. Legibility is a prerequisite of brush writing, but not a measure of its artistic value. The availability of five major script styles, and the natural variability of the soft brush give plenty of free reign to the creative impulse.

Painting is the art of creating visual illusions which point to invisible truths. It is intelligible because our eyes play tricks on us, and because it points to something

Fig. 3-25

beyond itself. Ambiguity is an important element in art. A simple twist of the line can make a man's face suddenly appear as a woman's body (Fig. 3-25). Art often exists in the twilight zone, where one thing can suggest or appear as another. The difficulty in Shodo is that the artist is caught between the spontaneity of creative deviation, and the discipline of legible language. Sometimes a slight change in stroke angle or direction can result in an error, or even in an entirely different character (Fig. 3-26). However, this is usually only a problem in fully cursive script, and even that is governed by a manageable number of rules.

Fig. 3-25

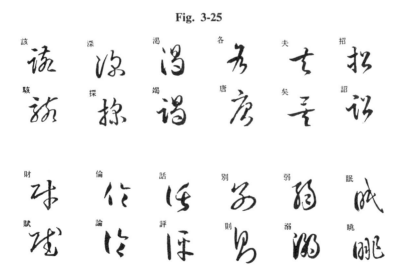

The attempt to accurately perceive a character and physically reproduce it with the brush is a unique type of intelligence test. Although a complex relationship of strokes make up the written language of *kanji*, there is no test score, and really no one right answer. An exact reproduction is impossible. There is no way to cheat, for the brush does not lie. It is so sensitive in fact, that some researchers in Japan are using the brush in the early detection of senility and disease. Through a scale sensitive to pressure, the movements of the brush can be transferred to a computer screen, and analyzed for signs of wavering, micro-fatigue, or split second loss of control. Like a seismograph, this instrument detects the early tremors in the human frame which bear warning long before the ground shakes.

Unfortunately, spatial intelligence in our society may be on the decline. Excessive television watching has been blamed, for it lulls the viewer into passivity, and impoverishes the imagination with its relentless barrage of rapidly shifting and disjointed images. Between the years 1960 and 1980, the Educational Testing Service in Princeton, New Jersey, found a significant decline in the national test scores of spatial intelligence. These tests presumably measured geometric recognition, three-dimensional visualization, and reasoning skills. We might obtain less formal measures of the decline by seeing what has happened to the quality of animation in children's cartoons, or by noting the reduced interest in hobbies of modeling and construction during that same period. Schools have steadily reduced their offerings of mechanical drawing and industrial arts, due to lack of student interest. Many professions require spatial intelligence and visual skills. Unless something is done to reverse the decline in these skills, there could be a serious impact on the future of fields like architecture, engineering, landscaping, or even surgery.

The spirit of any civilization is always reflected in its art. By studying the best of the past, we can revive the present, and bequeath something of even greater value to the future.

Principles for Giving Dimension to the Flat Surface

Life at the surface is dull, flat, uninspiring. We need creative insight to see the nuances and depths of things, and insight begins with perception. But inspiration is like the breath that we draw, all around us yet so easy to overlook. It is more comfortable to take for granted that which we see, and many willingly go through life with blinders. We can survive without being creative, but not much more. The cost of unimaginative existence is a life which is predictable and standardized, a life within the limits. In Shodo, the principles for giving dimension to the flat surface are:

1. **Saturate the Brush, with Restraint.**
2. **Minimal Pressure, Maximal Effect.**
3. **Fast on the Straight, Slow on the Curve.**
4. **Consider Figure and Ground.**
5. **Maintain Proper Stroke Angle and Distance.**

Chapter 4

Finding the New in the Old

The Reflection in the Mirror

An old Chinese expression says that we see in other people the reflection of our selves (Fig. 4-1). In Japan, the mirror has long been considered to have sacred properties. It faithfully reflects what is before it, and has much to teach to the person who is willing to look. The old character for mirror (*kagami*), has a second meaning (*kan ga miru*), which means to think or reflect on a model (*tehon*). This meaning is very close to that used in calligraphy, where the student learns by copying a model, either a photograph of an original masterpiece, or one done by the teacher. The *tehon* is usually an excerpt of a classical work, interpreted by the *Sensei*, or at least drawing on elements that the teacher has picked up over years of study. The student learns by copying the *tehon* repeatedly, trying to bring to life as many elements of the original as possible. Over years of practice the student is gradually given rank, and eventually teaching responsibility. You learn best by mirroring the teacher's work, and then sharing what you know with others.

Fig. 4-1

Other people are the mirror of ourselves.

This process of imitation leads to discovery. Each time you try to copy the *tehon*, you are caught by your own limited perceptions. This is a mildly frustrating process at first, because the brush is so difficult to control. The hand seems unable to reproduce what the eye sees. But in fact, the hand is reporting very accurately what the eye sees. We are poorer observers than we would like to admit. Only after a period of concentrated practice does the eye begin to discover the important details and proportions which were there all along. This comes as a surprise, a kind of *satori*, or awakening of the senses. This discovery is the beginning of real learning, and the excitement is often enough to propel the student into an enthusiastic period of practice.

Obviously you should select a *Sensei* who is technically skilled with the brush, but you are very fortunate if you can find a teacher who also has a fine character within. Ideally, the teacher should be one who has never stopped learning. The way of the brush is so wide and long that no one could ever exhaust its possibilities. Anyone can gain technical skill after a few years of practice. However, in evaluating a teacher you should look beyond the *tehon*, and ask what the art has done for the person behind the brush. We need not imitate other people to improve ourselves, but we can emulate the positive features of anyone we meet. Shodo gives us intimate access to the minds of many great individuals who lived centuries before us. By copying the works of the masters, we gaze into the mirror of the past, and try to recover our own genius. The deeper our dialogue with works of excellence, the greater becomes our repertoire of expression.

There is a special knack to being original. Being creative is easy if there are no standards. It is important to study the masterpieces of classical calligraphy to understand what true quality is. But no matter how good the copy, after all it is only a reproduction. The difficulty lies in being original, with excellence.

Maintain a Spirit of Relaxed Concentration

It is impossible to be yourself unless you are relaxed. As long as you are trying too hard for a certain effect, there will be a false note in your bearing. But it is also impossible to realize your potential without concentration and the effort to improve your self. The person who stops learning quickly stagnates in self-satisfaction, and is soon rejected by others. Relaxation and concentration appear to be incompatible only because people misunderstand the meaning of both. Coordination of mind and body allows you to relax and concentrate simultaneously. The important point is that concentration is a mental function, while relaxation is a physical one. Many people get it backward by trying to tense the muscles to concentrate, and slacken the mind to relax. This is a very unnatural state, and only further divides the mind and body. The mind works better when it is alert and focused. The body functions best when it is relaxed and calm. Though it is easy enough to accept this principle intellectually, it is almost impossible to use the brush properly without it. Coordination of mind and body should be considered a prerequisite to creative work, for without it both the artist and his work become unbalanced.

All too often in the interests of creativity, artists fall into narcissistic and highly subjective forms of expression. When the average person is unmoved by the artist's personal statement, it is easy to resort to snobbish statements in self-defense. In Japanese, there is a distinction drawn between individuality (*kosei*) and eccentricity (*kuse*). True originality is an inborn quality, while idiosyncrasy is a result of forced pretense. Though posing as liberated and free, eccentrics are often bound by their own standards of conformity, and may cling to them more stubbornly than the conformist.

Your character will mature of itself if you learn to relax completely and deepen your mental focus, and it will be your own. Raise your standards by using *tehon* that you consider worthy of emulation, and in time your brush writing will develop its own original character.

Expand Your Visual Vocabulary by Copying the Masters

In order to express yourself well in any medium, you need to master the vocabulary as well as the instruments of the art. Gestures will not carry you far in a foreign language. Even the masters of musical improvisation have behind them a good deal of experience in reading musical scores. Great masters of the visual arts, from Michelangelo to Picasso, had years of training in good representational drawing. The ability to make an accurate copy is not the end of creative work; it is a prerequisite to it. Rejecting this difficult phase of development deprives you of access to excellence. On the other hand, stopping at technical mastery, without developing anything original dooms your work to anonymity. Even commercial artists achieve success in their fields only by doing something truly original or outstanding. Few people make their living as artists, and even fewer achieve distinction for original work. Nor is this goal even practical for the average person. But creativity is by no means limited to the arts. Anyone can benefit from the ability to see the obvious through fresh eyes, and the capacity to show it to others.

It is difficult to be creative in the abstract. We need a focus. In calligraphy, the *tehon* gives us an artistic challenge of manageable proportions. It takes less than a minute to make a single copy, and even half an hour of practice can be rewarding. Still, making a good copy is no easy task, for the brush faithfully records every error in your perception. The rhythm and proportions of good calligraphy are so refined, that they immediately remind us how rough and rushed our daily life has become. After a period of concentrated practice, we come away a little better person. Spending time with a good book may have the same mental effect, but the brush adds a physical and visual dimension that reading alone lacks.

Some might object to the notion that copying can lead to creativity. The copy is a rehearsal, not a performance. It is not meant for display. A good artist has the skill to make a good copy, as well as the originality to create something new. A poor artist considers copying to be beneath him, when in fact it is beyond him. The purpose of trying to replicate the *tehon* is twofold: to train the eyes to notice what is in front of them, and to train the hand in a wider repertoire of strokes.

Truly creative work comes later, when you attempt to transfer elements of the old into the new.

Calligraphy is a learned skill, and involves physical maturation as well as practice. For this reason, the *tehon* produced for children and beginners often consist of a few, relatively simple characters, highly legible and straightforward (Fig. 4-2 a and b). The simplicity of a beginner's *tehon* is deceptive. It takes a

Fig. 4-2a   **Fig. 4-2b**

Fig. 4-3a **Fig. 4-3b**

great deal of skill and control to produce the master copy to begin with. Copies made by Japanese children are notably crude in comparison, although they may be very good for their age and skill level (Fig. 4-3 a and b). The brush writing of an adult beginner may resemble that of the child at first, though it is unlikely to have the child's sense of spontaneity. The adult is apt to be self-critical, and more self-conscious than the child.

Fig. 4-4

The questions on an intelligence test often give hints of what to look for in the answer. In Shodo, few hints are given. You must simply paint what you see. Once errors are pointed out they become obvious: misplaced or missing strokes, lines which should touch but do not, intervals which should be equal but are not. Perhaps the student's copy is not well centered on the page. Its internal spaces may be cramped, or an important stroke may be weak. If the piece is well executed, or has outstanding features of its own, variations from the original are tolerated, even encouraged. In fact, two accomplished *Sensei* may produce somewhat different *tehon* working from the same original model (Fig. 4-4).

Be Original, Not Just Different

Sonkatei (A.D. 648–703), one of the great Chinese masters of calligraphy, wrote at length on the process of creativity. He described three stages to learning the Way of the Brush. In the first stage you strive, like a baby, to learn shape, form, and position; and constantly have the feeling that you cannot quite get it right. In the second stage, you seek individuality and self-expression. At this level you have enough skill to have fun and be creative, but your artistic growth may be stunted by conceit. Stagnation eventually leads to a decline in ability. Only if you keep growing do you enter the third stage, where you are again as a small child, but

Fig. 4-5

Fig. 4-6

now having overcome pride and bad habits. Indeed the work of some of the masters does have a child-like quality, spontaneous and free of pretense. The work of Zen Masters Hakuin (Fig. 4-5) and Ryôkan (Fig. 4-6), both have this quality, and are very difficult to copy well. In fact, they do not make good *tehon* for the beginner. The person lacking in technical skill too easily confuses childlike, with childish. Many adults fall into this trap, trying to recapture the lost spontaneity of childhood, instead of seeking a higher spontaneity on the other side of maturity. There are no shortcuts to creativity, and by going back, they only create a caricature of the child that they once were.

You are never too old or too young to be creative, but you may miss it altogether. You are not likely to get it in school, and few people are lucky enough to work in a place which encourages it. Some people succeed in creative achievements, but many do not. If you stop learning you may even lose the urge to create. Creativity depends on your own initiative. In the practice of Shodo you are given a few guidelines, but mostly expected to find your way by trial and error, with occasional advice from the teacher. How much ink to apply to the brush? How much pressure? How fast or how slow to paint? You must ultimately answer these questions through your own experience. There are so many features which compete for your attention: line thickness, stroke beginnings, proportion, position, speed, endings, angles. It is almost impossible to get all of them right in one attempt. Sometimes one stroke out of twenty will be outstanding, while the rest are mediocre. We remember famous people for their successes, but their biographies often point to a long string of failed attempts along the way. The professional is more controlled and consistent, but like the beginner, is still learning all the time through trial and error. The best thing to do is mentally focus on one feature or principle at a time. Gradually you assimilate each one, and refine your corrections until they become very subtle and automatic. At this stage the student learns to control the brush without thinking about it, and can copy or deliberately vary the expression as he likes.

You may know that practice makes perfect, but do not confuse repetition with practice. If trial and error is to achieve anything, it requires sustained effort toward a goal or model of excellence. Without the desire to go beyond yourself, repetition only reinforces bad habits, putting you in a rut. An eccentric style may draw attention for a while, but it has no power to go beyond itself. Practice to improve, not just to repeat.

Find Something New in the Old

The artist makes an effort to express things which most people take for granted. The successful artist puts universal human experiences and aspirations into a tangible form. This figure has the power to reflect, recall, and even intensify the original impulse, so that others can understand and identify with it. The greater the talent of the artist, the greater the value and esteem of the work, though some artists are born ahead of their time. Paul Valéry said that no artist ever finishes his work, but merely abandons it. The non-artist is the same, except that he abandons it at a much earlier point, or does not even try. The weaker the creative impulse, the easier it is to give up on an idea. Then it becomes easier to let someone else do it for you. Why decorate life with ornaments, when you can renew it with art?

The impulse to create may come from anywhere, but it must take a legible shape to qualify as art. To create something new, we need to do more than just copy what we have seen. Once the character or subject has been selected, ideas and hints may be drawn from *tehon* or from reference books which contain classical works.

Fig. 4-7	Fig. 4-8

Then begins a searching cycle of mental and physical rehearsal, until you achieve the variation that you are looking for. The original impulse may come from the outside world, or it may be inspired by a notion from within. The character for the word (*moeru*), meaning "to burn," may be written legibly, and still bear a resemblance to living flames (Fig. 4-7). In Zen Buddhism, the Universe is considered essentially beyond description (*mu*). Though this character can be written legibly, it reflects associations which are themselves beyond words (Fig. 4-8).

In both cases the character is used as a vehicle to build momentum and lead the viewer beyond itself. It is difficult to achieve this effect by copying a *tehon*, although it may give you some ideas. Once you get an inspiration, you begin to grasp the essence of form. But in order to transcend it, you must find something new in the old.

Link Together Elements That No One Else Has Seen

Brush writing is bound by the conventions of legibility, most of which were developed for efficiency in reading and writing. However, brush painting must be enjoyed as well as understood. If everyone were to write characters in the same way, there would be no calligraphic art, only pretty lettering. With this in mind, we should devote some time to deliberately deviating from the *tehon*, or even painting without one. The art of ink painting (*sumi-e*) is another subject altogether, for it involves not letters but pictures, of landscapes, flowers, animals, insects, and other impressions of nature. It would appear to be simpler and have fewer rules than the Shodo, but the use of the brush and principles of composition are just as rigorous. The pictorial character of *kanji* is quite compatible with *sumi-e*. It has long been a common practice to show painted letters superimposed on a picture, from ancient scrolls to modern travel posters (Fig. 4-9 a and b).

In Oriental thinking, there is a twilight realm between letters and pictures, in

Fig. 4-9a   **Fig. 4-9b**

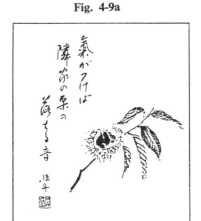

which one gradually fades into the other. You can select a *kanji* representing something in nature, and try to paint it as a picture rather than a character. Using a natural object, image, or photograph as a *tehon*, you can experiment with a number of variations on how to write the character. Each variation should be legible. The intent is to make a readable picture. For example the character for flower (*hana*) can be written to look like a flower arrangement (*ikebana*), using a photograph or drawing as a *tehon* (Figs. 4-10 through -13). There are details in the picture which lend themselves to portrayal as strokes in the character. The brush can be used to highlight petals, stems, leaves, or even parts of the vase. What makes this calligraphy and not *sumi-e* is that is still obeys the rules of legibility and stroke order, while at the same time allowing for some poetic license.

Fig. 4-10a

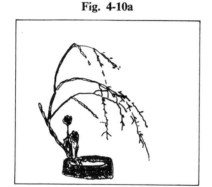

Fig. 4-10b

Fig. 4-11b

Fig. 4-12b

Fig. 4-12a

Fig. 4-13b

Fig. 4-13a

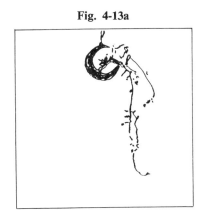

Since everyone looks at a picture in their own unique way, painting a character in this way almost guarantees that you will link together elements that no one else has seen. Giving a visual description of an object that others can see as well, you open a window on another way of looking at the world. The tangible reality of the object and rules regarding the written character compel you to see the object the way others might. A work of art is born at the interface between the subjective and objective points of view. There are as many points of view as there are people, so an exhibition by many artists on the same theme can be quite intriguing. Each work is unique, though all of them say the same thing.

The Fine Line

The first rule for creative work is a knowledge of the best of the past, which prepares you to pass something of value along to the future. The visual vocabulary of Shodo has developed over centuries of experimentation. Like the architecture of the past, it tends to fit the era in which it was born. The buildings that we live and work in are usually architectural variations on old themes. Calligraphy has developed in much the same way. It is impossible to create an effective break with the past without an intimate familiarity with tradition. But familiarity is more than just knowledge of facts, figures, names and faces. Perceptive awareness of the past must lead to intuitive vision of the future.

Creating a new variation is like trying to translate poetry into a foreign language. A faithful translation may not be beautiful, nor a beautiful one faithful. The challenge is how to keep the meaning without losing the poetry, a task which is so difficult that it compels many serious students to learn a foreign language, just for the pleasure of reading a work in the original. Since this is not practical for most people, there must be a more direct way to gain access to the poet's mind. This can be done through calligraphy, where the poem involves the entire mind and body, and leaves a vivid visual impression.

It takes some years to develop your own artistic style. If you push the rules of legibility and spatial balance too far, the brush strokes look sick and unbalanced (*byô-hitsu*). There may be a very fine line between genius and abnormality, but you have to draw the line somewhere. As Kenneth Rexroth said, art is the reasoned derangement of the senses. It takes a good observer, with an excellent sense of dramatic timing and expression to play a role well, and still be able to return to one's real self. A real fool cannot play the part of a fool on stage. The actor who cannot distinguish the difference in daily life is finished. Control is the safety valve which prevents the real derangement of the senses. In calligraphy, this control is provided by continued reference to the masterpieces of the past.

The second rule for creative work is good space dynamics. This depends on the energy and rhythm of the brush, in other words on the mind and body coordination of the artist. A work of art which lacks this energy is little more than dirty laundry, an unwanted glimpse of the subconscious. It may draw attention, but it will not be remembered. It requires a tremendous wellspring of internal energy to sustain creative work. This can be detected in the internal spaces of a character, which are extremely important to the life of the *kanji*. If the brush passes too close or deposits too much ink, the white space between the strokes may be sealed off. If the presence of nearby strokes is ignored, the work looks limp and lifeless. There is a heightened awareness when one stroke approaches another, as palpable as compressed air.

The third element of creative work is to overcome bad habits (*kuse*), and develop true originality (*kosei*). Individual freedom has been one of the great issues of the twentieth century, but nonconformity is not the answer. The point is not simply to be different or to defy authority, but rather to have something special to offer. We often do not realize the degree to which our habits enslave us, but there is always a day of reckoning. Dostoevski said that the second half of a man's life is made up of the habits which he acquired in the first half. Creative work can help you break old habits by renewing yourself. In the effort to achieve the right effect you may repeat the work dozens of times. There is nothing wrong with this, except that in repetition, you tend to lose the creative tension and expectation of the original attempt. Art is born, not manufactured. The freshness of the work tends to fade with familiarity and fatigue. Sometimes the first attempt produces the best work in a series, though the power of the work is not always obvious at the time. Good calligraphy gains power after the ink dries, becomes more interesting with repeated viewings.

Lastly, if it is to qualify as calligraphy, the work must be legible to the trained eye. Free form expression may qualify as art, but not as Shodo. The rules of legibility are covered in detail in the next chapter. They have been developed through centuries of experimentation, and represent the most efficient way to write and abbreviate the *kanji*. You cannot make up your own rules of spelling and grammar, just because you do not like standard English. Nor can you ignore the rules of legibility in Shodo. These rules do not make art, but they keep us on the right side of the fine line.

Principles for Originality with Excellence

Originality is not so mysterious, once you realize how it works. One of the best kept secrets of originality is that of not revealing your source. All artists do it, as do politicians, businessmen, and public speakers. Franklin D. Roosevelt said that the only thing we have to fear is fear itself. What most people do not realize, is that the same thing was said before him, in virtually the same words, by Francis Bacon, the Duke of Wellington, and Henry David Thoreau.

Real creativity is more than surreptitious plagiarism. It is the art of recognizing the universal in the particular, and saying the same thing in a different way. No two human beings are alike, yet fundamentally we have more in common than we have apart. At its best, art develops individuality and at the same time reinforces our sense of commonality. By emulating the better qualities of others you expand your own creative repertoire. One day you will find yourself free to stray from the original and pursue your own path. Whether your effort leaves a mark, how much it entertains, inspires, or enriches other people, is a measure of your creative success. To be creative with excellence:

1. **Maintain a Spirit of Relaxed Concentration.**
2. **Expand Your Visual Vocabulary.**
3. **Be Original, Not Just Different.**
4. **Find the New in the Old.**
5. **Link Together What Others Have Not Seen.**

Part II: The Changing Forms of Character

"If you want to paint a bamboo, as you take up the brush, you must create a living bamboo in your heart, until you can actually behold it with your eye."

—Soshoku (1036–1101)

Chapter 5

Visual Literacy in Japanese

Reading the Written Word

Vincent Van Gogh produced oil painted copies of Japanese woodblock prints, which were accurate in every respect except one. Van Gogh apparently made no attempt to replicate the artist's signature and place name, although these were perfectly distinct and beautifully brushed in the original Japanese print. He simply hatched it out as an abstract design, bearing little resemblance to the original (Fig. 5-1). Early Japanese oil painters did the same thing in painting the Western-style edifices first built in Yokohama. The details of the buildings were carefully portrayed, but the Roman Numeral foundation dates were painted like a random series of chicken scratches. There was nothing wrong with the eye of the artist in either case, he simply choose not to look closely at the letters.

Fig. 5-1a

Fig. 5-1b

There is ample evidence to suggest that the way that we see the world depends largely on how we have been taught to look at it. Psychologists and anthropologists have found that people of different cultures actually see the world differently, by highlighting and focusing on different aspects of their environment. Vision is apparently as much a matter of values and imagination as it is light and color.

Brush calligraphy is a visual art drawn along literary lines, a perfect unity of drawing and dialogue. But it appeals more to the eye than to the ear, and there is no reason to shy away from it because you cannot read what it says. The prospect of memorizing thousands of abstract symbols with arbitrary pronunciation is enough to turn anyone back from the start. In fact, it takes years of concentrated study for a Westerner to be able to speak, much less read and write Japanese at a practical level. Language fluency should be considered a goal compatible with, but entirely separate from the study of calligraphy. A great number of people who are fluent in the language, including many native speakers, have no ability whatsoever to paint characters with a brush, or even to read cursive scripts. It is also perfectly possible to write good calligraphy without being able to translate what you have written. Brush writing is a visual language, just as music is an auditory one, both of them expressing words in a medium other than ordinary speech. Recognizing this fact will remove the most difficult mental barrier that you face in attempting to appreciate the art of Shodo.

Like music, Shodo has its own rules of notation and expression. Notes organize sounds into music, and strokes organize lines into characters. These symbols have meaning and pronunciation, which adds an important dimension to the work, but if that were sufficient then it would not be necessary to use a brush. The translation and pronunciation are usually provided as a footnote or caption to the work. To fully appreciate the work, it is more important to be able to recognize and reproduce the combinations of strokes. Recognition is a matter of spatial awareness, which in calligraphy is reduced to three important elements: basic stroke combinations, balance, and shape.

Learn the Basic Radicals, or Building Blocks of the Character

Chinese characters, or *kanji*, are composed of combinations of strokes. A small number of strokes are used to produce all of the characters in the printed, or *Kaisho* script. The word *Kai* comes from the leaves of the *Kai* tree, which grow in exquisitely parallel intervals along the branch. This tree is said to represent the teachings of Confucius, and one of the only specimens of its kind in Japan can be found on the grounds of Yushima Seidô, the Confucian Shrine in Tokyo (Fig. 5-2).

The basic strokes of *Kaisho* are the *ten* (dot), *tome* (stop), *hane* (spring), *harai* (sweep), *ore* (fold), *magari* (curve), and *sori* (arch). These strokes are deceptively difficult to master, and each are produced by a unique use of the brush (Fig. 5-3).

Fig. 5-2a

Fig. 5-2b

Fig. 5-3

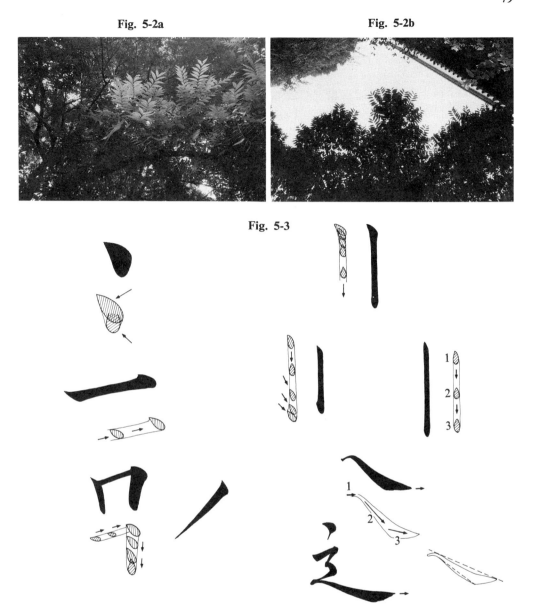

It is usually considered more productive to practice them in the context of the character itself, as they are never written in isolation.

The basic building blocks of the characters are known as radicals. They are classified by the position which they occupy in the character: *hen* (left part), *tsukuri* (right part), *kanmuri* (upper part), *tare* (upper-left part), *kamae* (outside part), *kutsu* (lower part), and *nyô* (lower-left part). The most common radicals are classified and named in Fig. 5-4, written in the *Kaisho* script. These need not be memorized, but you may wish to practice identifying a few from an excerpt of a famous classical piece of calligraphy (Fig. 5-5). Once the radicals of the characters become familiar they tend to stand out, like the face of a friend in a crowd.

Fig. 5-4

Hen (left part)

Har-vest	Tree	Heart	Ice	Cow	Hand	Earth	Going	Person
禾	木	忄	冫	牜	扌	土	彳	亻
秋	林	情	次	牧	持	地	行	休
税	枝	性	冷	物	折	城	後	供

Wo-man	Jewel	Cloth	Child	Rice	Hill	Ani-mal	Cloth-ing	Altar
女	王	巾	子	米	阝	犭	衤	礻
妹	理	幅	孫	精	防	猫	初	社
好	球	帆	孤	粉	降	狩	被	神

Hen (left part)

Moon	Money	Eye	Sun	Mouth	Rock	Direc-tion	Foot	Stand
月	貝	目	日	口	石	方	足	立
服	財	眠	明	吹	砂	旅	距	竣
朕	贈	睦	昨	呼	確	旗	路	端

Horse	Speech	Gold	Arrow	Moun-tain	Thread	Fire	Tomb	Bow
馬	言	金	矢	山	糸	火	歹	弓
駐	詳	銀	知	岐	終	煙	殊	弘
駒	詩	鏡	短	崎	給	焼	残	張

Tsukuri (right part)

Empty	Action	Hand	Strength	Container	Seal	Slope	Measure	Sword
欠	攵	又	力	斗	卩	阝	寸	刂
欲	政	友	効	料	却	郎	封	列
歌	教	取	動	斜	即	郡	射	到

	Page	Brush	Root	Bird	Strike	Hair	Axe	
	頁	聿	艮	隹	殳	彡	斤	
	須	律	限	雄	段	形	斯	
	領	筆	艱	雅	殿	彩	新	

Kanmuri (upper part)

Net	House	Rain	Bamboo	Hole	Grass	Lid	Roof	Cover
罒	𠆢	雨	竹	穴	艹	亠	宀	冖
罪	今	雲	第	空	若	交	安	冠
置	倉	霜	答	究	茂	京	家	軍

					Tiger	Age	Pick	West
					虍	耂	爫	西
					虎	老	妥	要
					虚	孝	采	覆

Kamae (top-cover)   *Tare* (upper-left part)

Receptacle	Country	Box	Cover		Individual	Sickness	Tent	Cliff
囗	凵	匸	冂		尸	疒	广	厂
固 圍	凶 函	近 区	同 岡		居 屋	病 痛	序 庭	原 厚
Vapor	Gate	Wrap	Wind					
气 気 氛	門 開 聞	勹 句 包	几 風 凪					

Nyō (lower-left part)   *Kutsu* (lower part)

Official	Road		Shell	Altar	Water		Dish	Heat
廴	辶		貝	示	水	心	皿	灬
廷 建	近 迷		責 賀	票 祭	泉 泰	忘 思	益 盡	無 然
Holding	Run							
夂 処 咎	走 起 超							

Fig. 5-5

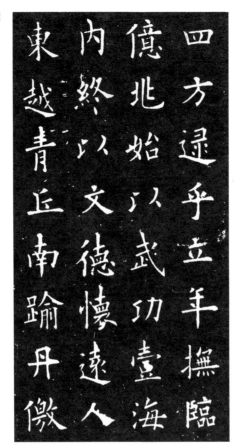

Find the Visual Center of Gravity of the Character

Balance is something we have to contend with from the moment that we take our first step. Once we learn to walk, we tend to take balance for granted. But balance is not an exclusively physical phenomenon. We also experience psychological and aesthetic balance. *Shodo* is an excellent way to improve your visual sense of balance. Every character has a center of gravity. When the weight of the character is poorly distributed it looks all wrong. If the sense of balance is not in your bones, it will not appear on paper either.

This is something which comes with experience, but there are certain guidelines

Fig. 5-6   Fig. 5-7   Fig. 5-8

that will keep you on track. Parallel horizontal strokes should be kept at equal intervals. This creates a sense of order and predictability, which is one of the crowning marks of the *Kaisho* script (Fig. 5-6). The center should be properly aligned. Not all characters are symmetrical, but they should be balanced on the center line. This provides a feeling of stability (Fig. 5-7). The left and right side

Fig. 5-9   Fig. 5-10   Fig. 5-11   Fig. 5-12   Fig. 5-13   Fig. 5-14

radicals, the *hen* and the *tsukuri*, should be written at about equal width (Fig. 5-8), although the right hand radical is often longer than the left, protruding both above and below it (Fig. 5-9). This is not always true, for sometimes the tops of the two radicals are aligned, and their bases are uneven, which creates an asymmetrical balance (Fig. 5-10). When the radicals are vertically aligned, the top one often rules, either by the base growing narrow (Fig. 5-11), or by the top forming a cover (Fig. 5-12). Here again there are exceptions, as when a long piercing horizontal stroke gives the character a kite shape (Fig. 5-13). A few *Kaisho* characters are also drawn on a slight diagonal, which gives them a sense of forward motion (Fig. 5-14). These are only general guidelines for *Kaisho*, but the visual center of gravity is always important.

Picture the Character in Its Geometric Profile

While the relationship of the radicals gives the character internal consistency, its outer shape gives it an overall identity, and helps establish its relationship to the characters which surround it. The contrast of various shapes and sizes give a column of characters a sense of majesty, like a procession in review. Each character contributes to the harmony of the whole, and not one detracts attention from the others. True to its Confucian association, *Kaisho* calligraphy reflects an intense social discipline, perhaps a distant reflection of the mentality of a feudalistic Imperial Dynasty. In this sense it is possibly incompatible with the modern mentality, but it reminds us of the strength which is possible in a harmonious social fabric.

Fig. 5-15

Some characters are easier to write well within a circular outline, while others are more at home in a triangular or off-set rectangular shape (Fig. 5-15). Visualizing this imaginary fence around the character can help prevent your arm from misplacing the critical first stroke of a radical.

This makes it easier to place subsequent strokes in their proper position. This imaginary profile helps you simplify the pattern, and keeps each radical in proper proportion to the whole character.

Learn the Proper Stroke Order through Repeated Practice

The stroke order is like a recipe for writing. It represents the most efficient way to write a character. There are only two basic rules of stroke order: from top to bottom, and from left to right. These are illustrated in Fig. 5-16, although there are occasional exceptions. The easiest way to learn stroke order is practice writing characters until it becomes second nature. After your hand becomes accustomed to the repeated patterns, a stroke written out of order feels wrong; much as a mistake in grammar jars your ears, even if you cannot cite the specific rules behind it. When in doubt, you can always consult a dictionary about the proper sequence.

Fig. 5-16

Left to right   Top to bottom

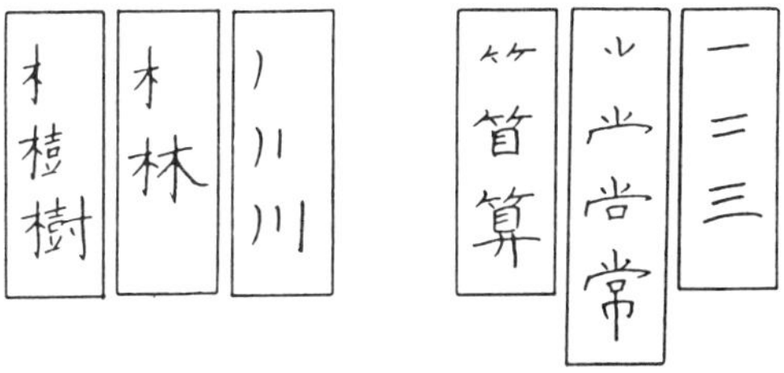

Once the ink is dry, how does anyone know the actual order in which the strokes were written? You cannot tell very accurately with a pen or pencil, but the brush makes it more obvious. The higher the quality of the ink, the more transparent the path of the brush. Once a stroke is made, any later stroke which passes over it actually appears to go under it. This gives the character a layered, three-dimensional effect, which is often preferred for works on exhibit. This effect is only possible with hand-ground *sumi* (Fig. 5-17). Even with less transparent ink, a trained eye can retrace the

Fig. 5-17

Fig. 5-18

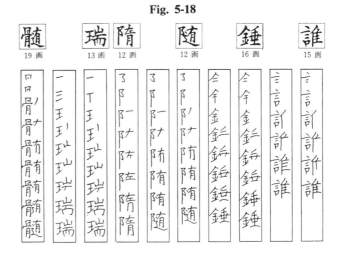

path of the brush by the trail and taper of the strokes. In any event, an incorrect stroke order is likely to interrupt the flow of energy between strokes. So it is better to form good habits early, than to try to break bad ones later on.

There are dictionaries of handwriting which illustrate the stroke order for every character, step by step (Fig. 5-18). It is not as complicated as it appears, because there are few exceptions to the rule, and the same patterns are repeated over and over again. The advent of the *kanji* word processor has meant that fewer and fewer Japanese people have opportunities to actually write their own language by hand. While the country has a nearly 100 percent literacy rate, young people are increasingly ignorant of the basic rules of stroke order.

To use a Japanese dictionary, you must either know the pronunciation of the character by heart, or reference it by counting the number of strokes. This is a cumbersome and time-consuming process, and trying to inspect the tiny print can be hard on your eyes. There are shortcuts for guessing the pronunciation, in that certain radicals routinely dictate the pronunciation of the character. This leads to a cornucopia of homonyms, words which sound the same, but have entirely different meanings. To confuse things even further, many characters have multiple readings, some of which were borrowed from the Chinese language and some of which are native to Japan.

Advanced technology has made it easier to look up characters using a word processor. You simply type in the desired word by pronunciation, and the characters come up on the screen. Since many characters share the same pronunciation, sometimes you get the wrong character. This seldom happens, because they come up in order of common usage, but if it does you just keep pressing the key until the right one appears. Obviously, in order to use a *kanji* word processor, you must be able to recognize the character on the screen. You need not know how to write it, but you must be able to read it.

It may seem to be a terribly slow and inefficient writing system which uses up to a dozen or more strokes to write a single character. However a Japanese writing at normal speed can write just as quickly as a person writing the same text in a Western language, sometimes even faster. A single character in Japanese may contain a concept worth several words in English. Moreover, daily correspondence is usually written in an abbreviated semi-cursive script. Using a word processor, you can type out a compound several characters long in little over a second. *Kanji* are not phonetic, but the Japanese are unlikely to abandon their present writing system in favor of

Fig. 5-19

a phonetic approach. For a language in which several dozen characters may share the same pronunciation, a phonetic alphabet would be a disaster.

Another important element of Japanese writing is the sequence of the characters themselves. The traditional sequence, and the general rule for calligraphy, is that characters are written in vertical columns from top to bottom, beginning at the upper right. There are exceptions to this, even in classical Chinese calligraphy, where occasionally the characters were written horizontally, from right to left. Most modern Japanese printing and business correspondence has adopted the Western convention of horizontal text from left to right, however Shodo retains the traditional style. *Kaisho* script can be written horizontally, because each character is written independently in block style. But cursive scripts which connect one or more characters must be written vertically. The letters were originally designed to flow in a certain direction. It would be as impractical to try to connect *kanji* horizontally, as it would to write cursive English script vertically.

The best way to simplify all of this is to practice writing a few columns. Several examples are provided, which show how the strokes can be practiced with a pen or pencil, using a *tehon* that was originally done with a brush (Fig. 5-19).

Put Verbal Literacy into Proper Perspective

Professional singers often learn to sing in several foreign languages, without being able to carry on a conversation in any. Of course they study the meaning and proper pronunciation of the song which they will perform, but it is not necessary to become fluent in a language to sing in it. Similarly, it is not necessary to learn Chinese or Japanese in order to enjoy or write good calligraphy. Because much of the poetry used in Shodo is written in classical Chinese or Japanese, even native speakers begin as beginners.

It is quite possible to enjoy calligraphy without actually practicing it. Many people enjoy music without learning an instrument. The participants get more out of it, but there are always more people in the audience than there are on stage. Even the knowledge contained in this book will put you ahead of the average Japanese who is untrained in calligraphy, in spite of the language barrier. Do not let lack of verbal literacy hold you back. Concentrate on learning to see the characters rather than read them.

Visual Culture vs. Verbal Culture

Many Westerners experience frustration in trying to deal with the Japanese on their own terms. Explanations of cultural differences may satisfy the intellect, but they are not very practical in the real world of business. Rules of etiquette and behavior are like rules of grammar: they work best when they come naturally. Interpreters are notorious for translating the speaker's words literally, and missing the real meaning or intent behind them. Understanding a people's way of thinking well enough to communicate effectively requires that you put yourself in the other person's place. The fastest way to do this is to find a way to penetrate the verbal surface, and make yourself appear as one of them. When the feeling of foreigness is gone, the communication barriers fall away of themselves.

It takes a long time to become fluent in the Japanese language, and few professionals in other fields have the time to even come close. A little knowledge can even backfire, because you may not be able to follow through. There is a shortcut. Try to appreciate the culture or master some aspect of it. A knowledge of calligraphy can be useful, because many of the same principles apply in the other arts as well. If you develop any degree of skill in the art, it will certainly be noticed and respected by any Oriental friends or associates, because so few people take the time.

Understanding the Way of the Brush can help you appreciate the practical use of certain Oriental aesthetic concepts: face, consensus, the emphasis on the group, and the importance of discipline and hard work. Most importantly, it will give you a way to participate in a visual rather than strictly verbal view of the world. Western culture has traditionally placed a stronger emphasis on logical thinking and verbal contracts. The Japanese can do this too, but they are more at home with visual thinking and implied agreements. We see ambiguity, insincerity, or unfairness in trade relations, and feel that we have a basis for complaint. However the Japanese view the same behavior from a different perspective, and may see us as equally unmanageable. There is an art to non-verbal communication, and it has a long history in Japan. It may be worth studying this art before we draw premature conclusions based on our own cultural criteria. You may find that the same principles which improve your calligraphy also facilitate your acceptance into Japanese circles, and that the barriers are more visual than economic.

Principles for Visual Literacy

Van Gogh saw the obvious and overlooked the subtle aspects of the Japanese woodblock print. We do the same thing when we view the world through our own biases. What do we see when we look at an object? Do we see the thing itself as it is, or do we put it in a category, and label it with a stereotype? To appreciate the unfamiliar we have to look at it with fresh eyes. But equipped with the knowledge of how to recognize the signposts we can go much farther. There is much to discover in the art of calligraphy. The principles then for visual literacy are:

1. **Learn the Basic Radicals.**
2. **Find the Visual Center of Gravity.**
3. **Picture the Geometric Profile.**
4. **Learn the Proper Stroke Order.**
5. **Strive for Visual, Not Verbal Literacy.**

Chapter 6

Image Training and Practice in Calligraphy

To Learn by Heart, Learn by Hand

The Chinese philosopher Chuang Tzu expressed the Taoist idea of learning as something beyond the reach of words. The wheelmaker braces the rim, sets the spokes, and centers the hub to make a near perfect circle, but cannot explain to others how this is done. Instead he says, the knack must be grasped by the mind, and learned by hand. This was also the rationale of apprenticeship, in which the craft could only be mastered through long years of experience, a system which fit the social order of the day. But what really took place in the transfer of learning from master to student? Is there something in this that we can still apply to our experience today? Are there advantages to a system which emphasizes learning with the body?

It has become apparent in many professions that successful performance is as much a matter of mental practice as of actual physical rehearsal. Concert pianists, and even chess players often play in their heads. Japanese *Shôgi* is a complex variation of chess, which is widely played in Japan. The playing board is somewhat similar to Western chess, but the pieces are designated by ranks written in Chinese characters (Fig. 6-1). The pieces are not

Fig. 6-1

only capable of promotion, but captured pieces can be dropped behind enemy lines like paratroopers, making the game both complex and unpredictable. An amateur player of considerable rank was once challenged to a game by a professional whom he had met on a cross-country train trip. The amateur politely refused, saying that he did not have a board. The professional responded in mild surprise saying, "You need a board?"

An accomplished professional in any field can mentally retain astonishingly complex patterns of information, and reproduce them at a moment's notice. One major difference between the master and the novice is the quantity and quality of imagery stored in the brain. Master patterns of performance were polished and refined by persistent rehearsal. Often what separates the fast learner from the ordinary person is the amount and caliber of mental practice, which gives shape and power to the physical practice sessions. Sports psychologists have found that mental practice can sometimes improve performance as much as mere physical training, although the combination of the two is superior still. Actually the two are hard to separate. Doing is the thing, but it is possible to grasp the essence of a movement in the mind and refine it to improve our physical performance.

Combine Physical and Mental Rehearsal

Image training is not a substitute for action, but a companion to it. Like the ready stance of the sprinter, it focuses all of one's resources on a single goal. Effort will not carry you far if you lack a clear intention. It may even work against you. Psychologists speak of the Law of Reversed Effort, or the "backfire" effect of trying too hard. However it is not the effort that is the problem, rather it is the negative or unclear imagery in the mind which points you in the wrong direction. Without effort there is no progress. We simply need to be careful that we make efforts to be headed in the right direction.

How many problems in life stem from an inability to know precisely what we want, and a failure to act accordingly? Creative living requires that we refuse to accept things at face value, seek out the positive possibilities that are within our reach, and act to achieve them. The real knack of performance is image training. Unfortunately, there is a crisis of imagination in the modern world. There are men and women of action, as there are men and women of thought, but few people do as Henri Bergson advised: to think like a man of action, and act like a man of thought.

The images that fill our minds and dictate our behavior too often come to us in prepackaged form. We are rich in audio-visual technology, but poor in our innate image-forming capacity. If you lose the habit of walking, you risk an early decline in mental and physical powers. Similarly, if you lose the habit of drawing or writing, both of which help you observe through your hands, then you risk losing the ability to see and think for yourself.

In traditional Japanese arts and theater, outsiders were not permitted to observe practice sessions. Secrets were too easily stolen. Once initiated, students were expected to spend a period of time learning by watching the master and senior students. Apprentices were expected to learn by observation, imitation, and a humble attitude toward being corrected. Minimal verbal instructions occasionally punctuated long periods of practice, during which the student learned the appropriate methods by trial and error (*kufû*). Mastery was expected to take years or decades.

Since it is not practical to return to this system today, we need to see beyond its outer trappings and grasp its essence: that of combining physical and mental rehearsal.

Move from the Obvious to the Subtle

We have seen how the *inochi-ge*, the longest and most resilient hairs at the center of the brush, can be used to bring the full impact of the brush to the surface of the paper. The *inochi-ge* represents the center of gravity of the moving brush, and produces the contours of the stroke in its wake.

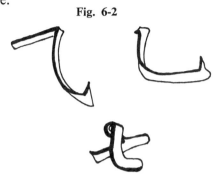

Fig. 6-2

The slightest articulation of the center of the brush can be used to produce all of the features of the stroke's outer shape. The path of the *inochi-ge* contains the secret recipe for the stroke itself. Those who can read it, can write it. The stroke contours are the obvious result of the more subtle path of the centerline of the brush. A slight hook, ripple, or accent in this life line is often all that is needed to recreate the impact of the original stroke. But this line is often so subtle that it can be missed in the blink of an eye. It can only be crudely diagrammed. The line does not always hug dead center, and may even cross the stroke from one side to another, like a skier changing direction on an uneven slope (Fig. 6-2). This gives the stroke a three, or even four dimensional appearance, reflecting the actual movement of the brush in space. Just as it is easier to walk than ski a difficult traverse, it is possible to ignore the challenging path of the *inochi-ge*, and still get through all of the strokes. But unless the brush is articulated with equal precision, the strokes will lack fidelity. The result will be a cheap imitation.

Maintain an Unbroken Flow of Ki

The thread of the silkworm is elastic and strong when drawn without hesitation, but easily breaks when the motion is stopped or suddenly jerked. The same thing can be said of the unwritten line which connects each of the strokes both on and off of the page. Like the line of the *inochi-ge*, it cannot really be diagrammed with accuracy, for it is more of a feeling in the fingertips than an actual line. It is also more obvious in the cursive styles of calligraphy, where most of the strokes taper off in the direction of the next stroke.

There is no rule which says that the brush must be moved in any particular way when it is off of the paper. In fact, it is often helpful to pause and mentally project the next sequence of strokes before you actually paint them. Going fast is no guarantee of going right. Trying to paint without pausing from beginning to end can cause you to miscalculate the placement of important strokes. Birds pause in flight without falling, but in suspension they never really stop. The wind grows calm, but air currents never really disappear. The secret is to tap into the under-

92

current of the movement, and never let it go. The line on paper ebbs, swells, and sometimes fades from sight, but it always comes back. The master brings it back with an unbroken flow of Ki energy from beginning to end, making the work appear as flawless as a seamless fabric. Wherever you look the line is unbroken. In the martial arts, this is known as a state of mind and body without any opening to attack.

The attempt to follow this line can be invigorating, exhausting, marvelous and frustrating. The *Ki-myaku*, or continuous line of Ki reveals all of your weaknesses and challenges all of your strengths. It is remarkable that some of the greatest masterpieces of calligraphy were simply the unrehearsed tidings of daily correspondence (Fig. 6-3). The brush of such masters was certainly as alive off of the paper as it was on it.

Fig. 6-3

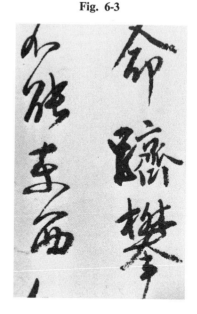

Learn How to Read the Calligraphic Score

A trained eye can follow the traces of the brush because it knows the movements of the hand. The best way to train the eye is through the hand, and this need not be done exclusively with a brush. Strokes can be traced with the forefinger, to the side of the work, or even on the palm of your hand. This not only helps you confirm the stroke order, but it coordinates eye and hand movements as well. It is a quick way to gauge proportions and shape without wasting paper, and can be done anywhere. All that you need is a copy of the score and a knowledge of the proper stroke order.

Fig. 6-4

The next step is to make a copy (*rinsho*) with a pen on unlined paper. You may wish to trace them at first, to accustom your hand to the movements and stroke order. But it is better to practice freehand, as tracing produces a lifeless copy. No artist ever learned to draw by connecting the dots. *Rinsho* with a pen is easier than with a brush, and makes a good dry run. It helps you make the transition from spectator to participant. Pen practice will sharpen your eye to the point where you can visually trace the lines, which will notably improve your appreciation of calligraphy. An example of pen *rinsho* for a cursive score is provided in Fig. 6-4.

To most Western people, *kanji* are an unfamiliar language, involving complex patterns that are difficult to make any sense of. Unless the image of the character is clear, image training is not much different from doodling. To an amateur, the conductor of an orchestra appears to be waving his hands at random. But a poor conductor can spoil a performance, and a concert without a conductor is likely to break down altogether. The brush is like the conductor's baton, and its use requires the same sense of precision and purpose.

Refine Your Movements as You Go

It is difficult to know how quickly to move the hand. To a certain extent you can gauge pressure by line thickness, and speed by the tone of the ink, but other variables also come into play. It seems natural to start painting slowly and deliberately, and speed up the strokes as they become familiar. In fact, it is actually better to practice painting quickly, and slow down a little as the movements become more refined. The genuine masters of any art always refine their movements as they mature. A talented young artist may be able to display technical virtuosity, but this is still an immature and potentially hazardous state of growth. In the martial arts, the stronger opponent makes the least movement. Real beauty is not flashy or conspicuous, it is the essential form which cannot be improved by further modification.

The beginner paints rather slowly out of necessity, in an effort to maintain control. Accuracy is important, but it is speed which gives the work a sense of vitality. But as you improve, hold a little in reserve. This will give your work the mark of maturity.

Image Training in Daily Life

Calligraphy is a superb method of image training, as are drawing, writing, music, and many of the performing arts. Despite the fact that economics, scientific, and technical fields may have gained greater social prestige in recent times, they still cannot compete with the humanities in the realm of the imagination. Most people agree that the arts are a good thing, but assume that they are secondary to the real business of life, at best a sophisticated form of entertainment. This may be true for the spectators of the arts, but the participants have a totally different inclination. The artist seems eccentric because of a preoccupation with that which cannot be seen. That much, the artist has in common with the fool. But while foolish fancy is content with vain and invisible imagination, the artistic impulse does not rest until it makes itself seen.

To use the imagination properly in life, we need to maintain balance of mind and body. The images that you hold in your mind have a direct impact on your posture, mood, and health. Does this mean that we should censor or reject any art which reveals human weakness? Not at all. Ignoring a thing does not make it go away. You can shut your eyes to something, but that does not necessarily shut it out of your mind. It is the way that we look at things which is important. Seeing things as they are does not mean being cynical, or dragging out the negative side of life. It is easy to fix and label things based on how they look. It requires more imagination to recognize their capacity for change, and to bring out their positive side for others to see.

Artists often become so wrapped up in their work, that they can no longer distinguish imagery from perception. Creative imagination requires that you become involved, but not that you be swept away. The world is full of souls who have drowned in whirlpools of their own making. To be creative you must be positive and poised, and not lose yourself in the process.

To be effective, image training requires relaxation. People who are overstressed often assume that relaxation is a matter of passivity and slack muscles. Remember that a drooping mouth is a sign of an empty mind. Real relaxation is not the absence of tension, rather it is the ability to act in any direction, without getting tired, confused, or lost in the process. It is the ability to live in the world without being distorted by it. If you cannot relax while you work, then how can you really relax away from work? What we need is poise, mental calmness and physical readiness under pressure.

When you are composed, you have a heightened ability to form mental images. Being adaptable, you can refine and apply them in action, moment to moment. In other words, you can improvise. It is easy to envy the uninhibited spontaneity of the person who seems poised under pressure. But whether in business or social life, or in a stage performance, the person who can improvise is one who has spent a great deal of time in mental and physical rehearsal. To some, this practice may be a matter of unconscious habit. But the majority of our behavior is controlled by habit, and any habit which was learned can be relearned.

Image training is a very effective way to change habits. The more specific the image, the greater the effect on our behavior. The best way to clarify your mental imagery is to put it into action. Various terms exist for this: role play, self-fulfilling prophesy, positive thinking. In plain terms it means giving it a try. Trial and error in the pursuit of a specific goal is nothing new, but nothing new can improve upon it. The problem is that in an effort to avoid error, people avoid trial. The result is that they end up procrastinating about everything important in life. It is easy to find excuses not to act, and you will always find a sympathetic ear.

Do not make the mistake of postponing action because your goals are not yet clear. It is better to move in some direction, and adjust it if it proves to be wrong. Experience is supposed to be the worst teacher, because it tests before it teaches. But only the procrastinators fail to learn its lessons, because they refuse to confront experience. The beginning driver overreacts to everything. With experience the reactions become more refined and automatic. The secret is to increase the frequency, but reduce the degree of adjustments until they become smooth and imperceptible.

Principles for Image Training and Practice

A Japanese proverb says that when the willpower is focused upon a stone, it can pass through it. There seems to be no limit to what the mind in action can accomplish. It is no coincidence that during periods of revival of the humanities and the arts, many men and women of genius achieved mastery simultaneously in several fields of endeavor. Imagination and action are not independent, they are one. If you want to get something done, ask a busy person. If you want to develop your imagination, emulate a creative one. The principles for image training and practice are:

1. **Combine Physical and Mental Rehearsal.**
2. **Move from the Obvious to the Subtle.**
3. **Maintain an Unbroken Flow of Ki.**
4. **Learn How to Read the Score.**
5. **Refine Your Movements as You Go.**

Chapter 7

A Picture Is Worth a Thousand Words

The Origin of *Kanji*

There are over 50,000 characters in existence, which over several thousand years have developed into more than a dozen script styles. Any attempt to cover this subject in depth would require several volumes. However, etymology is an important subbranch of calligraphy, and can add a further dimension to your study. For people who are not scholars of the language, the most important thing to know is that despite its complex appearance, the systems of Chinese and Japanese writing make sense. Not only are they inherently logical and well organized, but the use of *kanji* has several advantages over purely phonetic alphabets, and it works in the modern world.

As we have seen, Chinese letters (*kanji*) are composed of simple elements called radicals. Like musical notation, these radicals can be formed into a seemingly limitless number of combinations. Until recently, *kanji* were employed almost universally in the Far East. Like an Oriental version of Esperanto, it was an internationally understood written language. Originally developed in China, *kanji* were still in use in Vietnam and Korea until the end of the nineteenth century, and of course are still in use today in China, Taiwan, Japan, Hong Kong, and Singapore.

Most *kanji* are pictographic or ideographic. They are not read phonetically, and many have multiple readings which must be memorized. These readings vary considerably from one language to the next. Myth has it that *kanji* were developed in the age of the Yellow Emperor, by a four-eyed person who got the idea from observing the tracks of birds. But of course their real origin must be attributed to many people over the centuries. A chart illustrating the development of Chinese and Japanese scripts is shown in Fig. 7-1. It is not necessary to know all of the script styles to practice calligraphy, and many people choose to specialize in only a single one. However, a general knowledge of how they developed, and some practice of each of the variations can add more possibilities to your own style.

The Development of Script Styles

Kanji can be traced originally to the inscriptions etched by oracles on cow bones and tortoise shells (*kô-kotsu mon*), dating back nearly 3,500 years (Fig. 7-2). At the time they were probably used for divination. When they were first discovered

Fig. 7-1

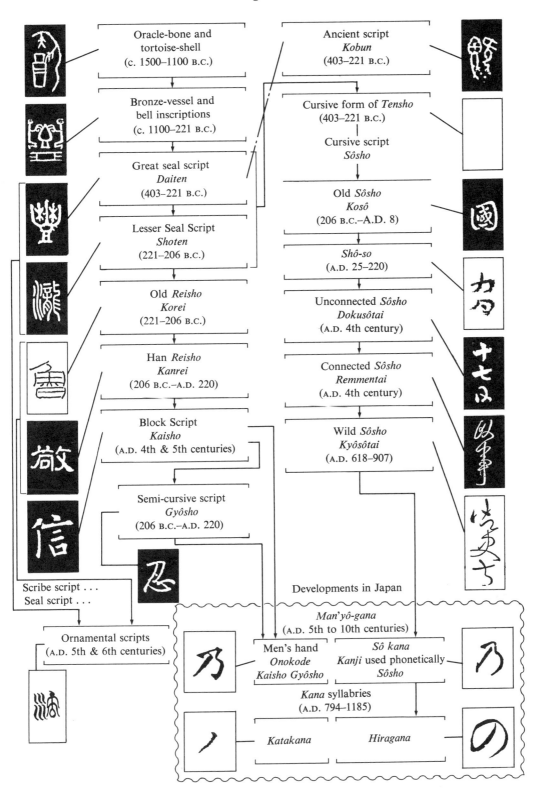

Oracle-bone and tortoise-shell (c. 1500–1100 B.C.)

Ancient script *Kobun* (403–221 B.C.)

Bronze-vessel and bell inscriptions (c. 1100–221 B.C.)

Cursive form of *Tensho* (403–221 B.C.)

Cursive script *Sôsho*

Great seal script *Daiten* (403–221 B.C.)

Lesser Seal Script *Shoten* (221–206 B.C.)

Old *Sôsho* *Kosô* (206 B.C.–A.D. 8)

Shô-so (A.D. 25–220)

Old *Reisho* *Korei* (221–206 B.C.)

Unconnected *Sôsho* *Dokusôtai* (A.D. 4th century)

Han *Reisho* *Kanrei* (206 B.C.–A.D. 220)

Connected *Sôsho* *Remmentai* (A.D. 4th century)

Block Script *Kaisho* (A.D. 4th & 5th centuries)

Wild *Sôsho* *Kyôsôtai* (A.D. 618–907)

Semi-cursive script *Gyôsho* (206 B.C.–A.D. 220)

Scribe script . . . Seal script . . .

Developments in Japan

Man'yô-gana (A.D. 5th to 10th centuries)

Ornamental scripts (A.D. 5th & 6th centuries)

Men's hand *Onokode* *Kaisho Gyôsho*

Sô kana *Kanji* used phonetically *Sôsho*

Kana syllabries (A.D. 794–1185)

Katakana

Hiragana

Fig. 7-2

Fig. 7-3

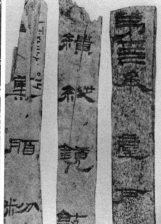

Fig. 7-4

Fig. 7-5

Fig. 7-6

only a little over a hundred years ago, many people took them as the natural markings on the bones of dragons. Whatever their original function, in time they were adopted for legal transactions, which were conducted by the exchange of appropriately marked wooden or bamboo strips (Fig. 7-3). These later came into official and religious use as bell inscriptions (Fig. 7-4).

From these inscriptions developed a non-standardized form known as the Greater Seal Script, or *Daiten* (Fig. 7-5). Many of the script styles which followed were invented by brilliant individuals, and adopted by the government of the period for official use. In the Ch'in Period, Li Ssu (210 B.C.) reformed and simplified the Greater Seal Script, and created the Lesser Seal Script, or *Shoten* (Fig. 7-6). These characters were designed to be of uniform size, and were widely taught in schools as part of an effort to unify the diverse tongues of a vast empire. The contemporary introduction of silk writing surfaces, inksticks, and brushes made the characters even easier to write. Li Ssu was said to have invented 3,000 characters, but by A.D. 200 there were over 10,000 in common use.

Around the same time, Ch'eng Mo, having been imprisoned for offending the Emperor, invented the Old Scribe's Script, or *Korei*. By straightening the curved lines and making the squares circular, he made the characters easier to write and more pleas-

Fig. 7-7   **Fig. 7-8**   **Fig. 7-9**

Fig. 7-10

ing to the eye. He also won back his freedom as a reward. Paper was invented during the Han Dynasty, during which the teachings of Confucius became official doctrine. This made it possible to reproduce these doctrines by hand. From the Han Dynasty *Kan-reisho* (Fig. 7-7), developed both the *Kaisho* block script (Fig. 7-8), and the semi-cursive *Gyôsho* script (Fig. 7-9). The fully cursive *Sôsho* script (Fig. 7-10) was not a further abbreviation of these two styles, but developed independently from cursive forms of the seal script. This helps explain why there is often little resemblance between the semi-cursive and fully cursive versions of the same character.

Fig. 7-11

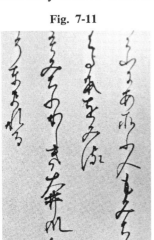

Sôsho is comparable to Western shorthand, and is only legible to those with special training in it. Writing skill and legibility were traditionally held in high esteem in China, and were often enough qualification to lead to an appointment to a high government post.

Chinese characters were introduced into Japan with Chinese culture in the Asuka (A.D. 552–646) and Nara (A.D. 646–794) periods. At first the Japanese used all of the Chinese styles, adopting many of the Chinese readings while adding many of their own. Some significant modifications were made in the characters themselves, including the development of three new script styles. From the fifth to the tenth centuries in Japan, the *Man'yô-gana* (Fig. 7-11), a highly cursive and ab-

Fig. 7-12

breviated form of *Sôsho*, was adopted for phonetic use as a kind of alphabet of Japanese, entirely apart from the original meanings of the characters. In an attempt to standardize usage, the many variations of the *Man'yô-gana* were eventually drastically simplified into the modern phonetic *hiragana* (Fig. 7-12), which was only standardized in the twentieth century. Today it is used in combination with Chinese characters, to help delineate pronunciation, and to express ideas in Japanese grammar.

The soft and feminine quality of the *kana* script was considered most suitable for a woman's hand, and was originally used by women for classical poetry, including the famous *Man'yô-shû* of eighth century Japan. The more articulate styles of *Kaisho* and *Ghôsho* were at first considered better suited to the male hand, and were used for official administrative and

Fig. 7-13

religious purposes. From these developed the *katakana* (Fig. 7-13), which were designed from parts of *kanji* written in *Kaisho* script. The *katakana* are also phonetic, and correspond exactly to the *hiragana*; except that today they are reserved for special uses, such as in telegrams, and to depict foreign loan words. They are rarely used in calligraphy. The distinction between the writing of the sexes was never made in China, and eventually faded in Japan as well.

The cursive and semi-cursive styles are covered in depth in the following chapter, and are only presented here as a background to the discussion of the etymology of *kanji*. One might assume that the earlier script styles would have long since been abandoned for their cumbersome impracticality. However, many of them are still in use in modern Japan, although mostly for decorative, professional, design, or artistic purposes. Many archaic script styles can be found in plaques, stone monuments, and in signature seals used in banking and business.

Rationale and Organization of the *Kanji*

Throughout history there have been attempts by brilliant individuals to organize the vast body of *kanji* which have come into common use. Though this study has an ancient heritage, the process continues today. During the Han Dynasty, a Chinese scholar named Kyoshin worked for 22 years, from A.D. 99 to 121 to compile an exhaustive dictionary, which is known as the *Setsumon Kanji*. Considered the Bible of *kanji*, it lists 9,353 characters and 1,163 variations, analyzing the etymology of every character in one or two lines of text. But by the Ch'ing Dynasty in the seventeenth century, over 40,000 characters were in use. In the mid-twentieth century a thirteen volume set known as the *Morohashi Daikanwa Jiten* was produced in Japan, listing 50,294 characters. Unfortunately, this massive work was destroyed during the wartime bombing, but it has been partially reconstructed from notes.

In Japan today however, there are less than two thousand characters in common use, compared to ten or twenty thousand in current use in China. In any case, it would seem to be an impossible task to memorize such a quantity of abstract symbols without a phonetic base. Yet according to Father Joseph R. De Roo, eminent scholar of Chinese *kanji* at St. Joseph's Friary in Tokyo, there are only six characters which can be said to be purely abstract. These are the characters for the numbers four through nine. All of the rest have a concrete, pictorial etymology, examples of which follow later in the chapter.

Although the characters themselves may have rather tangible origins, the system of writing itself was heavily influenced by divination and superstition. Kyoshin selected 540 radicals for his *Setsumon Kaiji*. This number was not chosen at random. In all things the Chinese sought a balance between the *yin* (odd, feminine principle) and the *yang* (even, male principle). The number 540 was considered an ideal number from the standpoint of Chinese numerology, because five plus four makes nine, which is the highest *yin* number; and this is balanced by a zero, which is a *yang* number.

Even when the system was modified, reference was made to numerology. In A.D. 1717, considering the need to organize the over 40,000 characters in use, a scholar named Kang Hsi reduced the number of radicals to 214, again a perfect number, because it contains one *yin* and two *yang* numbers, and the digits add up as follows: (2+1=3), (1+4=5), (2+4=6), (2+1+4=7), and so forth. The decision to standardize the number of radicals at 214 was more superstitious than rational, but it was not arbitrary. From the contemporary Chinese point of view of the Universal Order it made perfect sense. To have ignored such an important criterion would have been to invite disaster under Heaven.

More rational standards have been applied in subsequent efforts at simplification, striving for legibility and aesthetic balance. The average Japanese is no more aware of the roots of his own language than the average Westerner is of the Greek or Latin roots of his own. Often the modern meaning of the character is quite remote from its original pictorial associations. Some etymologies are quite interesting and make useful mnemonic devices. Instead of memorizing a dozen or more strokes in random array, it is easier to learn to associate familiar radicals in the form of a story or image.

Characters in modern use are of six basic types: pictographs representing shape or form (*Shôkei*); letters representing number, quantity, or position (*Shiji*); joint-radical characters combining two or more elements by meaning (*Kai-i*); ideo-phonetic characters which contain one part for meaning and one for pronunciation

Fig. 7-14 *Examples of Characters by Type*

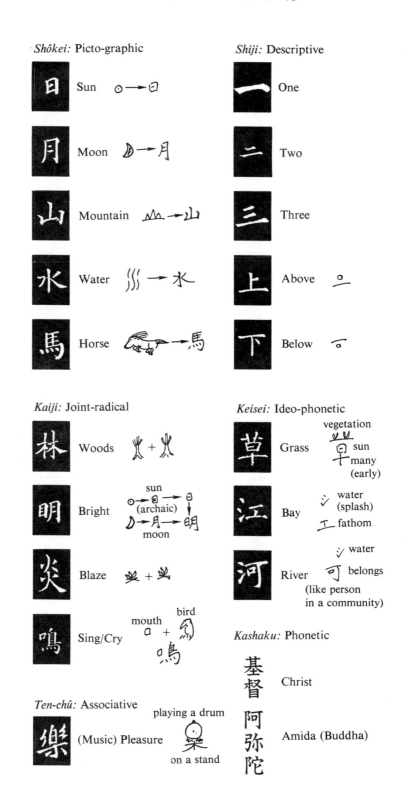

Shôkei: Picto-graphic

日 Sun

月 Moon

山 Mountain

水 Water

馬 Horse

Shiji: Descriptive

一 One

二 Two

三 Three

上 Above

下 Below

Kaiji: Joint-radical

林 Woods

明 Bright

炎 Blaze

鳴 Sing/Cry

Ten-chû: Associative

樂 (Music) Pleasure

Keisei: Ideo-phonetic

草 Grass

江 Bay

河 River

Kashaku: Phonetic

基督 Christ

阿弥陀 Amida (Buddha)

(*Keisei*); associative characters which draw on original connections to customs or related phenomena (*Ten-chû*); and pure phonetic affixations, which ignore the meaning, but use the common reading of the character to help pronounce a foreign word (*Kashaku*). The last type is mostly used in China, and is a nightmare of complexity, which the Japanese avoided by use of the relatively simple and phonetic *katakana* syllabary. Examples of each of the types are shown in Fig. 7-14.

Origin of the Phonetic Japanese Script

Although the modern use of *hiragana* and *katakana* have been standardized for both printing and handwriting, some styles of Shodo still make use of the *Man'yô-gana* script. It is not necessary to memorize all of the variations in common use, which make up an entire specialty of themselves, but it would be helpful to note the origin of each of the Japanese *kana* characters, and at the same time learn the basic pronunciation of the language.

Some of the *hiragana* reductions resemble the original *Sôsho* model and some do not, but in most cases there is at least a family resemblance. In Fig. 7-15 there is a chart of *hiragana* origins, which is greatly simplified, as there are in fact dozens of prototypes for each symbol. Special reference dictionaries list exceptional examples of these for calligraphers to use in improving their own work (Fig. 7-16). The

Fig. 7-15

(right to left) a, i, u, e, o, ka, ki, ku, ke

(right to left) ko, sa, shi, su, se, so, ta, chi, tsu

104

(right to left) te, to, na, ni, nu, ne, no, ha, hi

ひ	は	の	ね	ぬ	に	な	と	て
比	波	乃	祢	奴	仁	奈	止	天
比↓比↓ひ	波↓波↓は	乃↓乃↓の	祢↓ね↓ね	奴↓奴↓ぬ	仁↓仁↓に	奈↓奈↓な	止↓止↓と	天↓天↓て

(right to left) fu, he, ho, ma, mi, mu, me, mo, ya

や	も	め	む	み	ま	ほ	へ	ふ
也	毛	女	武	美	末	保	部	不
也↓や↓や	毛↓毛↓も	女↓女↓め	武↓む↓む	美↓美↓み	末↓末↓ま	保↓保↓ほ	部↓部↓へ	不↓不↓ふ

(right to left) yu, yo, ra, ri, ru, re, ro, wa, o

を	わ	ろ	れ	る	り	ら	よ	ゆ
遠	和	呂	礼	留	利	良	与	由
遠↓遠↓を	和↓和↓わ	呂↓呂↓ろ	礼↓礼↓れ	留↓留↓る	利↓利↓り	良↓良↓ら	与↓与↓よ	由↓由↓ゆ
								ん
								无
								无↓无↓ん↓ん

n

Fig. 7-16

Fig. 7-17

(right to left) a, i, u, e, o, ka, ki, ku, ke

ケ	ク	キ	カ	オ	エ	ウ	イ	ア
介	久	幾	加	於	江	宇	伊	阿
介 ↓个 ↓ケ	久 ↓ク	幾 ↓キ ↓キ	加 ↓カ	於 ↓オ ↓才	江 ↓エ	宇 ↓宀 ↓ウ	伊 ↓イ	阿 ↓ア ↓ア

(right to left) ko, sa, shi, su, se, so, ta, chi, tsu

ツ	チ	タ	ソ	セ	ス	シ	サ	コ
川	千	多	曽	世	須	之	散	己
川 ↓川 ↓ツ	千 ↓チ	多 ↓タ	曽 ↓ソ	世 ↓世 ↓セ	須 ↓ス ↓ス	之 ↓シ ↓シ	散 ↓サ ↓サ	己 ↓コ ↓コ

テ	ト	ナ	ニ	ヌ	ネ	ノ	ハ	ヒ
天	止	奈	仁	奴	祢	乃	八	比
天 ↓ テ	止 ↓ ト	奈 ↓ ナ	仁 ↓ ニ	奴 ↓ ヌ	祢 ↓ ネ	乃 ↓ ノ	八 ↓ ハ	比 ↓ ヒ

(right to left) te, to, na, ni,
    nu, ne no, ha, hi

フ	ヘ	ホ	マ	ミ	ム	メ	モ	ヤ
不	部	保	末	三	牟	女	毛	也
不 ↓ フ	部 ↓ ろ ↓ ヘ	保 ↓ ホ	末 ↓ エ ↓ マ	三 ↓ ミ ↓ ミ	牟 ↓ ム	女 ↓ メ	毛 ↓ モ	也 ↓ ヤ ↓ ヤ

(right to left) fu, he, ho, ma,
    mi, mu, me, mo, ya

ヲ	ワ	ロ	レ	ル	リ	ラ	ヨ	ユ
乎	和	呂	礼	流	利	良	與	由
乎 ↓ ヲ	和 ↓ ワ	呂 ↓ ロ	礼 ↓ レ	流 ↓ ル	利 ↓ リ	良 ↓ ラ	與 ↓ ヨ	由 ↓ ユ

(right to left) yu, yo, ra, ri,
    ru, re, ro, wa, o

								ン
								无
								无 ↓ ン

n

matter is much simpler for *katakana*, where sections of basic block *Kaisho* were adopted intact (Fig. 7-17).

For those who cannot read the Japanese syllabary, there is *romaji*, which is the romanized transcription of the Japanese language. Though it is commonly used, it is not a very accurate reproduction of the way that the Japanese people actually talk. A simple guide to the phonetics of *romaji* is provided in the Introduction, and may prove helpful in pronouncing transcriptions of Japanese words or poetry. Many books provide a Romanized rendition of Japanese terms and translations, so it is worth taking the trouble to learn.

Etymology in Perspective

There are a number of works available on the etymology of the *kanji*, but the best one in English is Father De Roo's *2001 Kanji* (Institute of Japanese Studies, Tokyo, 1980). It is a thorough and informative work on the etymology of the major characters in use in modern Japanese. The product of twelve years of research, this unique reference work is designed to be used by beginning students of the language, and it totally circumvents the need to count strokes or memorize character readings. A simple chart of stroke elements, more elementary than the radicals, leads you quickly to the character. The book provides a detailed, cross-referenced background of each word's etymology, meaning, and pronunciation. It is an ideal reference work for a Western student of calligraphy, although it was intended as a reading dictionary for foreign students of Japanese. Some of the word origins reveal inter-

Fig. 7-18 *Examples of Kanji Etymologies*
Descriptive

Sô, kuwa, mulberry tree: Many silkworms moving (又) on the mulberry tree (木).

Setsu, yuki, snow: type of rain falling from clouds (雨) which can be held in the hand (彐).

Kyô, kagami, mirror: metal (金) reflecting the face of a stranger (竟). The stranger makes sounds (音) like the temple bell standing (立) on two legs (儿) on the horizon in the sun (日).

Nyû, chichi, breast, milk: mother's hand (爫) holding the baby (子) to the breast (乚).

Fu, ukabu, float: mother's hand (爫) holding the baby (子) in the bathwater (氵).

Ban, yorozu, myriad: the numerous weeds (艹), which are like stupid scorpions hiding under a rock (禺).

I, kakomu, surround: enclosure (囗) around a well (井) to keep children and foreign objects from falling in.

Shun, haru, spring: sun (日) rising higher (夵→夫) with greater intensity.

Shi, ha, tooth: teeth close off or stop like a foot on the ground (止) the mouth (口), and are like unhusked yellow grains of rice (米).

Dan, kotowaru, set apart, refuse, apologize, give warning or notice: grains (米) stored in a corner (匚), and protected from outsiders by an axe (斤).

Tô, nigeru, flee, run away: moving (辶) as fast and far away as possible from the many (兆) people of high rank (儿).

Kô, hikari, light: flames (⺌) on a high podium (兀).

Fû, kaze, wind style, manner: bees are a superior (丿) insect (虫), which sound like the wind buzzing in a hive (几).

Sen, fune, ship: a junk with battened sail (舟), containing a family which has eight (八) mouths (口) to feed.

Chi, haji, shame: red ears (耳) indicate shame in the heart (心).

Nen, thought, feeling, idea, desire, attention: a feeling in the heart (心) concentrating on the present (今), as when you are eating (食).

Do, okoru, anger: resentful feelings (心) of an enslaved (奴) heart, like a woman (女) who must work with her hands (又).

Kai, natsukashii, nostalgic: heart (心) contains much feeling, like having many (ナ) pockets (mm) in the clothes (衣).

Bô, isogashii, busy: the condition of the heart (心→忄) which leads one to a heart attack and an early death with the lid (亠) on the coffin (L).

Bô, wasureru, forget: what is supposed to be in the mind (心) is now dead (亡) in a coffin (L) under a lid (亠).

Jaku, sabishii, lonely: unmarried young uncle (叔), feeling small (小) while still working (又) under the elder brother (上), in the family house (宀).

Ideas

Setsu, opinion, theory: words coming out of the mouth (言) of a self-asserting older brother with horns (兌).

Toku, eru, profit, advantage: make it a rule (彐→寸), to go (彳) like a peron walking (儿) to work at sunrise (旦), and you can make a living.

Shi, kokorozasu, aspire to, will, intention, aim: the mind and heart (心) of a professional man (士) who knows much (十) about a few things (一).

esting details of Chinese customs, while others offer profound insights into philosophical concepts. Fig. 7-18 provides a sampling of etymologies, to illustrate how the Chinese think in pictures. There is indeed a highly sophisticated method in the madness.

Rediscover the Beauty of the Ancient Script

The use of the brush for painting the early script styles differs somewhat from that presented in earlier chapters. Many of the earlier scripts were carved, not painted, and materials were comparatively primitive. Everything from the purpose of the writing to the cultural background was different from that which eventually evolved into the art of Shodo. Yet these ancient scripts still enjoy great

Fig. 7-19

Fig. 7-20

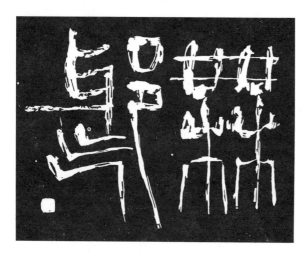

popularity among modern calligraphers, and even appear commonly in commercial art. The use of ancient and archaic scripts in modern life is far removed from its original purpose, but presents a remarkably modern impression when brought to life by an artist. Modern artists in the West have also drawn themes and forms from the primitive, giving us a sense of intimacy with people who were probably much like ourselves, but lived long ago.

The ancient scripts are usually presented in the form of brushwork (Fig. 7-19), wood carving (Fig. 7-20), or as artistic seal carvings (Fig. 7-21). Carving characters in wood or stone is a fascinating pursuit in itself, although it requires time and patience. In either case, the original model must be painted with the brush. If the brush work lacks vitality, it is unlikely that the carving will be any better. But whether you purchase, commission, or produce a carving yourself, it gives you a durable impression, from which you can find greater depth for pleasure or contemplation.

Fig. 7-21

Principles for Appreciating *Kanji*

Kanji are a key to what links many Asian cultures. They are a way of thought, a way of grasping and writing about the world in pictures. They are masterpieces of concise visual description, and they are beautiful to write and behold. They contain the aspirations and insights of several great cultures, and for that reason alone they are worth our devoted attention. But they are also the language of the brush, and a bridge to the mind of the artist. The way to enjoy them is:

1. **Study the Development of Script Styles.**
2. **Appreciate the Rationale of the *Kanji*.**
3. **Note the Origin of the Phonetic Scripts.**
4. **Put Etymology in Perspective.**
5. **Rediscover the Beauty of the Ancient Script.**

Chapter **8:**

Spontaneity Born of Discipline

The Unity of Opposites

Throughout the history of both East and West, ways of thinking have swung back and forth between an emphasis on spontaneity or discipline. Complex systems of political, economic, and social values often revolve more or less around the issue of control. In calligraphy, spontaneity may be defined as movement by natural impulse, free of outside interference; while discipline is movement which is trained or controlled. In theory, these concepts appear to be mutually exclusive. But in practice, one of them cannot exist without the other. Like right and left eye, their mutual presence gives depth to vision through perspective.

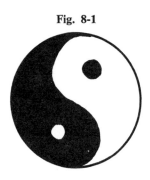

Fig. 8-1

As suggested by the well-known *yin-yang* symbol (Fig. 8-1), the extreme of one thing always contains within it the seeds of the other. This idea has been widely misinterpreted to mean that people should avoid extremes and seek a bland, temperate lifestyle. But in life or in art, who really wants to set the thermostat at a constant temperature? Real balance of *yin* and *yang* consists of the ability to go to the extreme without going over the edge. Figure skating would not be an art if it consisted entirely of going in safe straight lines or gentle curves. A good skater maintains perfect control in the most dangerous turns and leaps, and can build a sense of mounting drama in a simple forward line. What thrills and inspires is not the bland middle but the balanced outer limits; to exceed and surpass the ordinary, and still land with your feet on the ground. Freedom is often thought of in terms of lack of rules. But as Robert Frost said, writing free verse is like playing tennis with the net down. The presence of rules makes freedom possible.

On the other hand, freedom is often denied others by those acting in the name of law and order. Hitler described Winston Churchill as a fiery incendiary, who was bent on destroying all of Europe. Carl Jung called this a process of projecting the darkness in one's own soul outward to others, because of a refusal to face it within. It is facing the Shadow which brings it to the Light, not projecting it on others. Knowing that every front has a back, and that every light has a shadow, we should realize that we have a choice. The same glass of water can be called half-full or half-empty, depending on whether we choose a positive or a negative point of view. Both are true: the question is which do we choose? The attempt to hug the middle is a denial of both extremes, and often leads to its own excesses. The balance of opposites does not lie in the realm of mediocrity. It is easier to criticize others than to correct ourselves. Better that we find the balance of spontaneity and discipline within, before we find fault with the excesses of others without.

Many of the traditional Japanese arts have been influenced by the Zen idea of coming to terms with the dilemma of opposites through action, rather than philosophical discussion. The aesthetics of Zen gardening, architecture, and calligraphy all reflect practical and successful solutions to the problem of freedom and control. The Zen arts of Archery (*Kyûdô*) and the Tea Ceremony (*Sadô*) are both based on highly disciplined and formal rituals. Yet to watch one who is accomplished in the art is to experience a freedom of movement totally free of constraint. The immature beginner tries too hard to be free, and gets caught up in himself.

Even the seemingly free form arts of pottery and flower arranging achieve their pleasing effects through strict attention to aesthetic principles. Scientists tell us that the apparent randomness of events is underlain by a precise mathematical order. Practice in the formal styles of calligraphy can convince you that perfect order has a liberating effect, while the abbreviated styles give you a sense of the organic integrity of unrehearsed motion. The mature mind is not concerned with freedom or discipline as such, because it is centered at either extreme. In the Universe, the center is everywhere and the circumference is nowhere. The immature mind is always vaguely uncomfortable, because it is off-center wherever it goes.

Many people are drawn to the cursive styles of writing, because they seem less rigid and more spontaneous. But without discipline the abbreviated hand becomes careless. There are certain guidelines which you can follow to help preserve the integrity of cursive writing.

Reading the Abbreviated Hand

We have seen how each of the various script styles developed. *Gyôsho* is the semi-cursive derivative of *Kaisho*, whereas *Sôsho* developed independently as a fully cursive derivative of *Tensho*. While all styles ultimately stem from *Tensho* origins, their independent development led to some differences in stroke order and appearance. Even many Japanese are not aware that the *Gyô* and *Sô* scripts have independent ancestry, and many assume that one is simply a further abbreviation of the other. It is also commonly assumed that *Sôsho* is a free-style script, when in fact it has its own strict rules of legibility. Because it is rarely used in daily life in Japan, many people educated after the Second World War cannot read it at all. The Occupation forces mistakenly associated calligraphy with the pre-war fascist regime in Japan, and the practice of Shodo was outlawed for a period of time, during which much important knowledge was lost. Chinese people are more comfortable with the *Sô* script, and use from three to ten times as many characters in daily life as do the Japanese.

Fig. 8-2

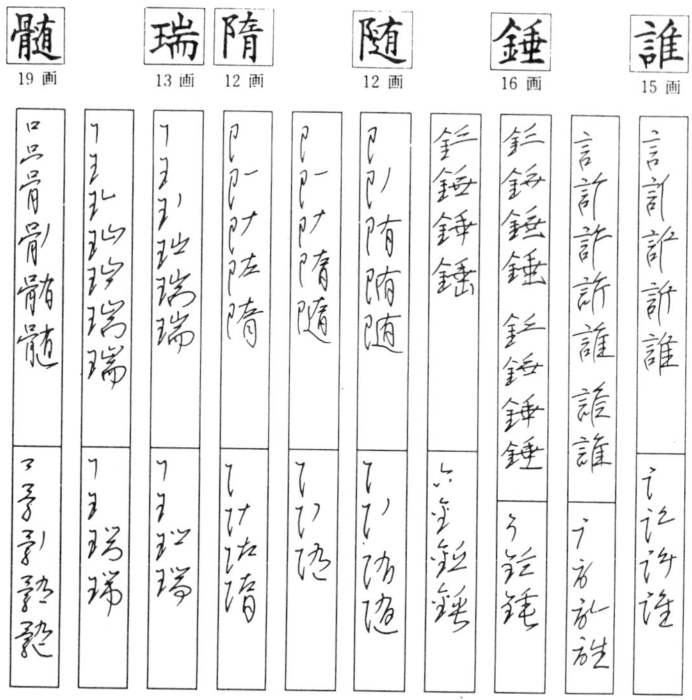

Sôsho script is not less formal, it is simply less familiar. However, because of the visual appearance and mental attitude adopted in writing the three major scripts, we will adopt the convention of formal, cursive, and abbreviated to describe the *Kai, Gyô,* and *Sô* scripts. Each style was developed for ease of writing, and was an improvement on its predecessor. In the cursive and abbreviated styles the path of the brush is often easy to observe because the connection between the strokes is clearly articulated. But the strokes often crisscross and overlap, making it difficult sometimes for the untrained eye to follow. As with *Kaisho,* there are dictionaries which illustrate the stroke sequence step by step (Fig. 8-2).

The consolidation of several strokes into one, and the clear liaisons between strokes allow the character to be written at greater speed, and give it a more dynamic interplay with the characters on all sides of it. The reason for the particular path of the brush may not be obvious to the eye, but with practice the hand usually finds it to be the path of least resistance. Practice in writing the strokes with a pen is the best way to understand why this is so.

In photography, as in calligraphy, there is a place for formal pictures. But for a formal occasion, people tend to strike a stiff and awkward pose. Candid moments are rare. There are more unguarded moments at a casual gathering, but not all people are equally photogenic. One person may look good whenever a picture is taken, while another always seems to get caught in the middle of a sneeze. The quality of charisma is not so much a matter of facial features as of personality. The cursive and abbreviated styles of calligraphy give a greater opportunity for casual expression and personality, simply because they appear less formal. But to appreciate their style, we need to learn to read the abbreviated hand.

In *Gyôsho* : Preserve the Qualities of Character

Although *Gyôsho* is cursive, it is still plainly legible. It is casual enough however, to give us a glimpse of the character behind the brush, as well as in front of it. What follow are excerpts of the great classics of *Gyôsho* calligraphy, with brief comments on the personal qualities of each.

Fig. 8-3

Elegance: O-gishi's *Rantei-jô* is considered the classic work of *Gyôsho* writing (Fig. 8-3). It may not appear unusual at first glance, but the more that you try to copy it, the more you discover how rich and subtle are its qualities. The vertical line undulates in a relaxed and luxurious manner. A variety of shapes parade themselves without repetition or self-consciousness, with all of the elegance of a good fashion show. The characters themselves seem to be swimming, pulled by gentle cross-currents. Strokes which usually touch in standard calligraphy, overlap and cut across other radicals in a friendly way in this work, but never cling.

Poise: O-gishi's *Shûgyô-no-jô* is very even by contrast, more poised and reserved (Fig. 8-4). The intervals between the characters are fairly regular, and the vertical line is well maintained. The horizontal strokes uphold a very consistent upward slant of about ten degrees, which gives the work a quality of steady optimism. The axis of each radical is slightly offset the vertical, being counterpoised to create a feeling of harmonious contrast.

Dynamic Strength: Gan-shinkei's *Sôza-ikô* is quite vigorous by contrast (Fig. 8-5). Many of the characters have a big-chested, bold appearance. They seem to magnify themselves, and project into the surrounding space, which is more crowded than in the previous work. The piece is fast-paced, one character following the other with a quick, strong pulse. The vertical line wanders freely, in some places almost colliding with the columns to either side, like a confident army on the march.

Fig. 8-4   **Fig. 8-5**

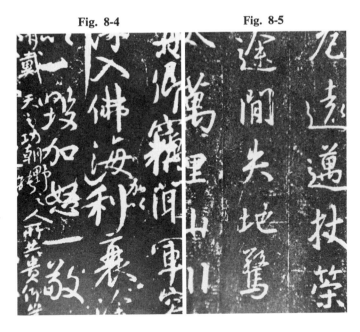

116

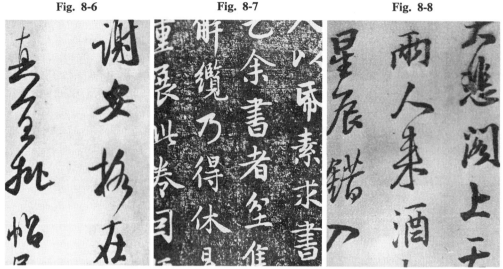

Fig. 8-9

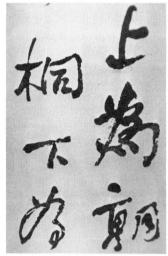

Fig. 8-10

Persistence: Beifutsu's *Ritai-Shijô* has a strong vertical line, a persistent willpower which is capable of connecting several characters in a single long stroke (Fig. 8-6). This rapid movement without break continues to the long tails and stroke endings which carry the task to the end, and beyond. Both in the individual characters and in the line as a whole, the sense of initiative is big and ambitious, growing more intense and compressed as it proceeds.

Internal Consistency: Chôsugô's *Rantei Jûsan-batsu* is steady and predictable, but shows a good sense of coordination (Fig. 8-7). Many like strokes repeat the same pattern, such as right diagonal sweeps, long horizontal strokes, and short dots. They maintain a theme, and like well-coordinated jewelry or clothing, create an overall sense of harmony. The characters are orderly and well spaced, but not overly rigid.

Originality: O-taku's *Hôkô Kichû-sho* brims with confidence and originality (Fig. 8-8). The vertical axis of the characters changes freely. Many are slightly distorted or exaggerated in one direction. They are too skinny, too tall, or have too narrow a base. They are gangly but strong, and move without a trace of apology. Corners are sharp, stroke beginnings are spirited, suggesting an inventive and original mind.

Self-Expression: Kashôki's *Gyôsho Sakketsu* is also original, but not as insistent (Fig. 8-9). The characters are exaggerated, but quite at home with themselves. Space is used very generously, with few characters for the space available, and full round strokes. There is a lack of pretense which reflects a refreshing sense of maturity.

Dimensionality: Kûkai's *Fûshin-jô* is a classic work, revealing tremendous depth of spirit (Fig. 8-10). The extreme contrasts of thick and thin, wet and dry strokes suggest distance and perspective. The work never repeats itself, moving from moment to moment with the deep breath of discovery. The energy of the work never fades, and shows a great capacity for self-renewal.

In *Sôsho*: Maintain the Continuity of the Line

The fully abbreviated hand may be less legible as writing, but it is more vibrant as a direct expression of the spirit. While *Gyôsho* has a social or communicative face, *Sôsho* is closer to the speed of thought, like a memo taken in shorthand. Of course it too must be legible, for what good is a memo which no one can read? But it must also contain the energy of the mind that moves the hand. What follow are excerpts of some of the great classical masterpieces of *Sôsho*, along with brief comments on what they reveal of the master behind the brush.

Fig. 8-11

Articulation: O-gishi's *Jû Shichi-jô* shows remarkable articulation for a script style which is this abbreviated (Fig. 8-11). The strokes are exaggerated, and clearly separated. The thickness of the line, and the even spacing of the characters suggests that the original work was done at a slow and confident pace.

Clarity: O-gishi's *Shogetsu-jô* by contrast, shows more speed and less articulation, but not at the expense of clarity (Fig. 8-12). The strokes are easy to follow. Despite a considerable display of virtuosity, we sense the ease and control of the master's brush. Two characters are repeatedly joined into one, but each retains its own distinct identity.

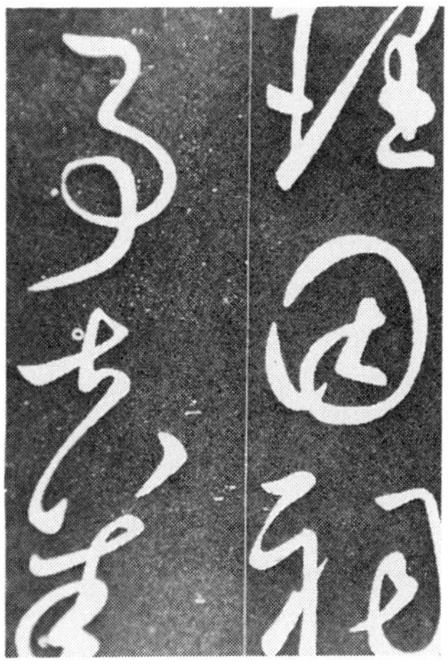

Youthfulness: O-kenshi's *Gendo-jô* is round and full, almost baby faced (Fig. 8-13). It brims with youthful vigor. Nowhere does the

Fig. 8-12   **Fig. 8-13**

118

Fig. 8-14   Fig. 8-15   Fig. 8-16

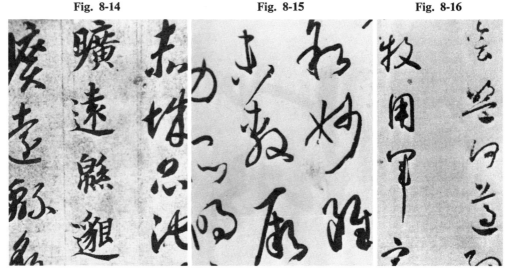

Fig. 8-17

line stick or drag behind. The internal space of the characters seems to swell out and exert itself within its youthful range.

Refinement: Chi-ei's *Shinsô Senjimon* is characterized by gradual transitions of exceptional refinement (Fig. 8-14). From thick to thin, large to small, tall to wide, sharp to round, like a finely woven tapestry each dimension gradually emerges into the next. There are no sudden transitions or surprises, but once the changes are made, they are unmistakable. We only notice the metamorphosis after it has happened. The continuity is further reinforced by a strong consistency in the vertical line, a sign of unbroken concentration.

Boldness: Sonkatei's *Shofu* is the opposite of Chi-ei's in many respects (Fig. 8-15). The vertical line shifts axis, not gradually but in clear steps, continuing the lateral shifts in bold strokes. There are daring contrasts inside each character as well. The emphasis in fact, is on the character itself, rather than on its relation to the characters around it. From start to finish, the work is strong and deliberate.

Calmness: Kaiso's *Sôsho Senjimon* is strong in the vertical line, like some of the previous works, but almost all of the characters are long and thin (Fig. 8-16). The vertical line is further emphasized by the wide margins between columns. The characters are well spaced and orderly, showing gradual transitions with no surprises. They speak to us from a height, with the wisdom and experience of the elderly.

Flamboyance: Kaiso's *Jijo-jô* is such a contrast to the previous work, that it is hard to believe they were done by the same person (Fig. 8-17). Kaiso's work is an excellent example of how a person can reach both extremes and come out ready to try again. Almost all of the characters in any one column are connected into a single continuous stroke. They spill out of every boundary that ordinarily contains a character. The lines are fast and free, but they never collide. Even when they venture into the adjacent column, it is in a daring, teasing way, always pulling back at the last moment.

Do Not Sacrifice Legibility

Though the outer appearance of the cursive and abbreviated scripts are quite different from the formal block style, they all make use of the same radicals, each of which has its own conventions for writing. In Chapter 5 we looked at the meaning and form of each of the major radicals in the *Kaisho* script. It may be helpful to compare the same radicals written in the *Gyôsho* (Fig. 8-18) and *Sôsho* (Fig. 8-19) scripts. Remembering that one is not necessarily a further abbreviation of the other will help account for the dissimilarities in some of the shapes.

Fig. 8-18

Hen (left part)

Har-vest	Tree	Heart	Ice	Cow	Hand	Earth	Going	Person
禾	木	忄	冫	牜	扌	土	彳	亻
秋	林	情	次	牧	持	地	行	休
税	枝	性	冷	物	折	城	後	供

Wo-man	Jewel	Cloth	Child	Rice	Hill	Ani-mal	Cloth-ing	Altar
女	王	巾	子	米	阝	犭	衤	礻
妹	理	幅	孫	精	防	猫	初	社
好	球	帆	孤	粉	降	狩	被	神

Hen (left part)

Moon	Money	Eye	Sun	Mouth	Rock	Direction	Foot	Stand
月	貝	目	日	口	石	方	足	立
服	賊	眠	明	吹	砂	旅	距	竣
朕	贈	睦	昨	呼	確	旗	路	端

Horse	Speech	Gold	Arrow	Mountain	Thread	Fire	Tomb	Bow
馬	言	金	矢	山	糸	火	歹	弓
駐	詳	銀	知	岐	終	煙	殊	弘
駒	詩	鏡	短	崎	給	焼	残	張

Tsukuri (right part)

Empty	Action	Hand	Strength	Container	Seal	Slope	Measure	Sword
欠	攵	又	力	斗	卩	阝	寸	刂
欲	政	友	劢	料	却	郎	封	列
歌	教	取	動	斜	即	郡	射	到

		Page	Brush	Root	Bird	Strike	Hair	Axe
		頁	聿	艮	隹	殳	彡	斤
		須	律	限	雄	段	形	斯
		領	筆	艱	雑	殿	彩	新

Kanmuri (upper part)

Net	House	Rain	Bam-boo	Hole	Grass	Lid	Roof	Cover
罒	个	雨	竹	宀	艹	亠	宀	冖
罪 置	今 倉	雲 霜	第 答	空 究	若 茂	交 京	安 家	冠 軍
					Tiger	Age	Pick	West
					虍	耂	爫	西
					虎 虜	老 孝	妥 采	要 覆

Kamae (top-cover)　　　　　　　　*Tare* (upper-left part)

Coun-try	Recep-tacle	Box	Cover		Indiv-idual	Sick-ness	Tent	Cliff
囗	凵	匚	門		尸	疒	广	厂
国 園	凶 函	匠 区	同 岡		居 屋	病 痛	序 庭	原 厚
Vapor	Gate	Wrap	Wind					
气	門	勹	几					
気 気	門 閉	句 包	風 凪					

Nyô (lower-left part)   *Kutsu* (lower part)

Official	Road		Shell	Altar	Water	Heart	Dish	Heat
又	辶		貝	示	水	心	皿	灬
廷 近			責 賀	票 祭	泉 泰	忘 思	盞 畫	無 然
建 逮								

Hold-ing	Run							
攵 処 発	走 起 超							

Hen (left part)

Fig. 8-19

Har-vest	Tree	Heart	Ice	Cow	Hand	Earth	Going	Person
禾	木	忄	冫	牛	扌	土	彳	亻
秋 税	林 枝	情 性	冷 次	牧 物	持 拶	地 珠	行 役	休 停

Wo-man	Jewel	Cloth	Child	Rice	Hill	Animal	Cloth-ing	Altar
女	王	巾	子	米	阝	犭	衤	礻
妹 好	理 球	幅 帆	孫 孤	精 粉	防 降	猫 猪	初 被	社 神

Hen (left part)

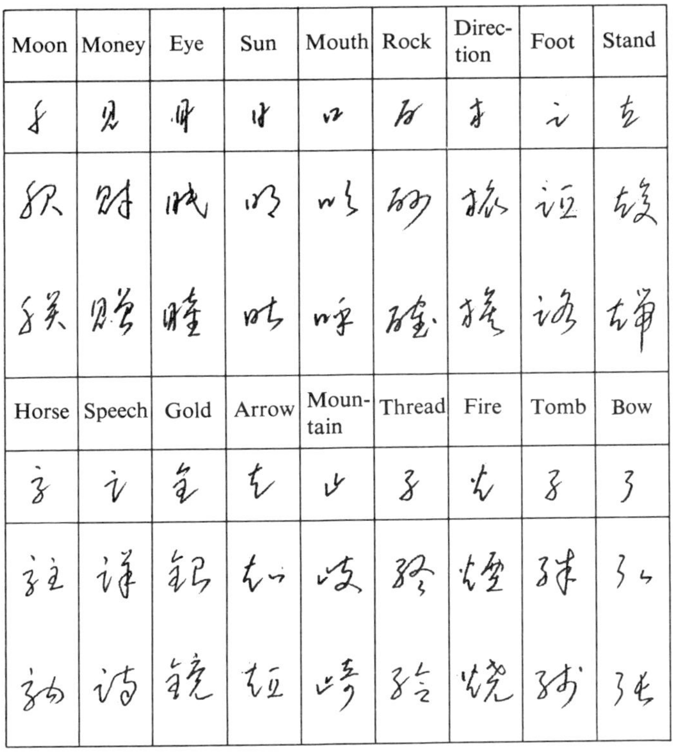

Moon	Money	Eye	Sun	Mouth	Rock	Direction	Foot	Stand

Horse	Speech	Gold	Arrow	Mountain	Thread	Fire	Tomb	Bow

Tsukuri (right part)

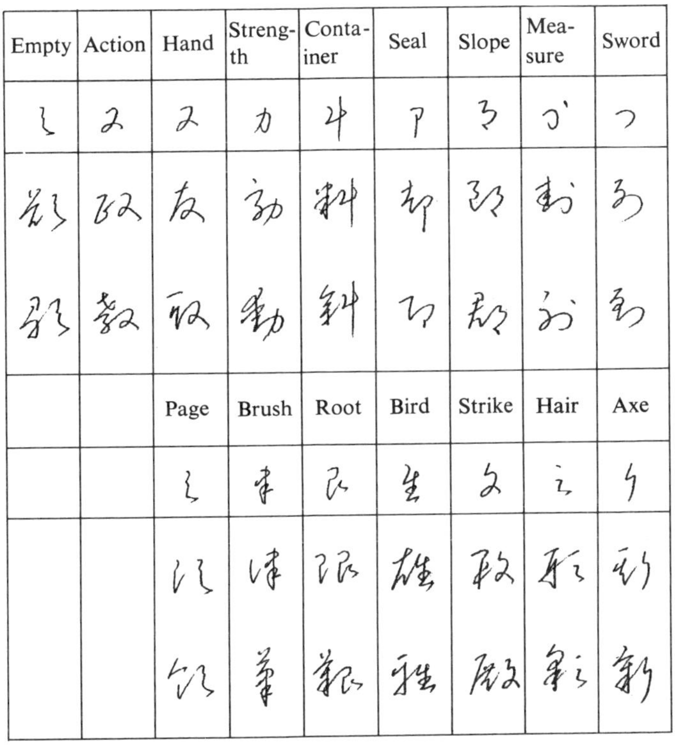

Empty	Action	Hand	Strength	Container	Seal	Slope	Measure	Sword

		Page	Brush	Root	Bird	Strike	Hair	Axe

Kanmuri (upper part)

Net	House	Rain	Bamboo	Hole	Grass	Lid	Roof	Cover
				Tiger	Age	Pick	West	

Kamae (top-cover)   *Tare* (upper-left-part)

Country	Receptacle	Box	Cover		Individual	Sickness	Tent	Cliff
Vapor	Gate	Wrap	Wind					

Nyô (lower-left part)   *Kutsu* (lower part)

Official	Road		Shell	Altar	Water	Heart	Dish	Heat
⌣	⌣		与	3-	小	⌣	Ƨ	⌐
達	占		責	零	泉	忘	盖	無
達	連		貸	祭	東	里	盍	然
Holding	Run							
及	也							
及	記							
及	超							

Use Space Generously

Stroke continuity is the most outstanding feature of the cursive and abbreviated scripts. The danger in intertwining strokes is that they easily become entangled. To prevent this you must use space generously, and not necessarily take the shortest path to the next stroke. There are various ways of doing this. You can go around, or enclose a liberal loop of space inside or under the character, or you can offset and separate strokes which in the *Kaisho* script would intersect. Other techniques include offsetting the relative height of adjacent radicals, or using asymmetry to balance several radicals around a common center (Fig. 8-20).

Gyôsho should create a sense of articulate movement, while *Sôsho* should invoke a sense of running or flowing, like water in a stream. You want to run, but not trip and fall. The best way to prevent a break in the continuity of motion is to preserve and use space generously. Like a window or door, it is the empty space

Fig. 8-20

Radicals of different
heights

Radicals on different axes

which makes it useful. It is easy to overlook or disregard that which we cannot see, but the secret of good calligraphy is that you *can* see space. It is a real palpable entity, like the air that we breathe, and just as important. The special privilege of the calligrapher is getting an opportunity to show it to others.

Script Styles in a Cultural Context

Fig. 8-21

Pagoda,
Hôryûji

When Chinese culture, along with Buddhism, was introduced into Japan during the sixth century, it came in the form of architecture as well as language and thought. It is not surprising that there should be a similarity between the two. The pagodas built during that period bear a strange resemblance to the *Reisho*, or Scribe Script which preceded it (Fig. 8-21). The curve of the stroke beginnings and endings call to mind the spreading layered rooftops of the pagoda. The concept of stacking rooftops makes more sense when viewed in the light of the stacking of horizontal strokes in a character.

Chinese culture was also imported to Japan during China's Sung Period, in the tenth and eleventh centuries. The Great

South Gate at Tôdaiji in Nara, Japan was heavily influenced by Sung architecture, and bears a likeness to the calligraphy of Beifutsu (A.D. 1051–1107), as shown in Fig. 8-22. Proportions of the two are similar, as is the contrast of thick and thin horizontal strokes. The *Sho-in* style of architecture, which started in Japan in the 1300s, seems close to the calligraphy of that period as well, with its thick strong

Fig. 8-22

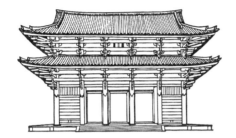

Great South Gate
(Nandaimon), Tôdaiji

Fig. 8-23

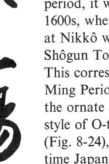

Kôjôin Guest Hall, Onjôji

lines and wide stable structure (Fig. 8-23). If Japanese architecture had a Baroque period, it was in the early 1600s, when the great shrine at Nikkô was built for the Shôgun Tokugawa Ieyasu. This corresponded to the Ming Period in China, with the ornate and articulate style of O-taku's calligraphy (Fig. 8-24), during which time Japan underwent

128

Fig. 8-24

Karamon, Nikkô

Fig. 8-25

another influx of Chinese culture.

Even today, the square, efficient style of lettering used in modern Japan is reflected in the slick, efficient buildings which are reshaping Tokyo's cityscape (Fig. 8-25). It may not make sense to try to restore the values of medieval culture, even if it were possible. But it makes even less sense to destroy and lose sensitivity to a great cultural heritage. As we shape our buildings, so they shape us. How much more so the language and letters which occupy our thoughts?

Buildings reflect the more formal and social aspects of our lives, but gardens and landscapes reveal the way that we see nature. Japanese gardens have much in common with calligraphy, and were influenced by many of the same aesthetic principles. You should no more run through a work of calligraphy than you would a garden. Both are designed with a crooked path, which forces you to slow down and notice the scenery. Rocks in a Japanese garden are chosen for their shape and proportion, and placed with great care. Like the strokes of the brush, once in place they cannot be moved. A column of characters is similarly arranged in a broken

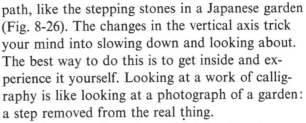

Fig. 8-26

Fig. 8-27a

Fig. 8-27b

path, like the stepping stones in a Japanese garden (Fig. 8-26). The changes in the vertical axis trick your mind into slowing down and looking about. The best way to do this is to get inside and experience it yourself. Looking at a work of calligraphy is like looking at a photograph of a garden: a step removed from the real thing.

We have seen how the vertical line is not always straight. Another analogy in the Japanese garden is the waterfall. A broken line always has more interest than a straight one (Fig. 8-27). There are unobtrusive hints of human habitation, such as latticework fences and small huts (Fig. 8-28). Everywhere you find the same harmonious proportions and skillful use of nearly parallel lines, just as you do in brush painted characters. Language is but one visible manifestation of the human spirit. It has many dialects in the arts and products of human culture.

Fig. 8-28

Principles for Abbreviated Writing

The meaning and pronunciation of the written word are extremely important. They are, after all, the main reason for writing. But anything written by the hand also bears the mark of human emotion, values, and culture. It is possible to mask your message in words, but not your character or culture. These emerge in spite of us, as subconscious revelations of ourselves. It is important to recognize and cultivate all of the dimensions of our talent. Personal experience is too limited by itself; but we can easily draw on the vast heritage that spreads in our wake. If a culture is ignorant of its roots and blinded to its potential, it will be forced to settle for the mediocre middle. Spontaneity and discipline are both needed to bridge the gap. Brush writing is a disciplined shorthand for spontaneous vision; one way of making sense of what we see. The principles for abbreviated writing are:

1. **Learn to Read the Abbreviated Hand.**
2. **In *Gyôsho*: Preserve the Qualities of Character.**
3. **In *Sôsho*: Maintain the Continuity of the Line.**
4. **Do Not Sacrifice Legibility.**
5. **Use Space Generously.**

Part III: The Aesthetics of Self-Transformation

"Words are the voice of the heart. Writing is a picture of the mind. By this we know the large-hearted, and by this we know the small-minded."

—Yôyû (53–18 B.C.)

Chapter 9

The Art of Enjoying Calligraphy

Developing Artistic Taste

It requires experience and insight to judge the quality of a work of art. Lack of familiarity with an artistic genre leads to misinformed judgments, based on inappropriate criteria. A Western tourist may be easily satisfied by a mediocre Oriental landscape painting. An Asian might have trouble accepting the exaggerated use of shadows in Western portraiture. Each sees the world, and therefore art, through the colored glasses of his own culture.

In the beginning, all you have is your own subjective likes and dislikes. People often find that as their taste develops, so does their evaluation of quality. Hopefully, the child who hates vegetables and loves candy grows into an adult with more sensible tastes. After a few years of study, you may easily change your mind about what is good in the art world. Until then, it is important to expose yourself to as much work of quality as possible.

The problem is that experience is not necessarily a guarantee of good judgment. History often proves the critics wrong. The best art critics of the day scoffed at the work of the early French Impressionists. They expressed their disapproval by sarcastically wiping their spectacles, as if what they saw was the result of dirt smudges, rather than deliberate dabs of paint. Renoir was railed as an idiot for painting nudes as if their skin were green. New styles in art are rarely appreciated at the time that they emerge.

On the other hand, not all new styles survive the test of time. The avant-garde artist often hides behind a smoke screen of ambiguous words, like the Emperor in new clothing. A lot of money exchanges hands in the art world by sleight of hand. How much more difficult to know quality when the art form is from another culture? The best way to refine your taste in calligraphy is to acquire a basic degree of background knowledge, wide exposure to the classics, and to practice yourself. At the very least you should learn enough not to hang the work upside down.

Respect the Conventions of Mounting and Display

Certain conventions are observed when a piece of calligraphy is produced for display or competition. The work is never truly finished until the seal of the artist has been affixed, and the calligraphy has been framed or mounted for display. Mount-

134

ing the work on a scroll preserves and protects the work, which otherwise may be subject to wrinkling, tearing, or dirt smudges. Unfortunately this can be an expensive process, requiring a good degree of technical skill. Scroll mounting is best left to a professional. However there are inexpensive temporary alternatives to display-

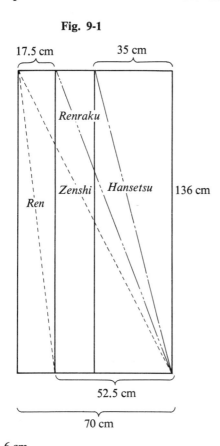

Fig. 9-1

ing a work, such as loosely attaching it to a scroll or hanging it in a frame, but these are considered quite informal.

Paper comes precut to standard sizes (Fig. 9-1). The largest size is called *Zenshi* (136 cm × 70 cm). Regular practice is done on *hanshi* (33.5 cm × 24.5 cm), about twelve of which can be cut from a single sheet of *Zenshi*; but the *hanshi* size is never used for formal display. *Zenshi* can be cut vertically to various standard widths, or horizontally to a not-quite-square rectangular shape, to produce the size used for exhibited works. Smaller sizes of the rectangular proportion are called *tanzaku*, while smaller sizes of the almost square shape are known as *shikishi*. Thick premounted paper is available in various sizes, but it is more expensive per sheet, and therefore not always suitable for practice. Premounted paper is more convenient and easier to frame, but it is harder to work with, and does not always give you the same delicate resistance as handmade paper.

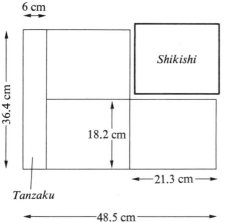

For the aficionado, there is a fantastic range of materials in brushes, ink, and paper. One can buy brushes made with peacock feathers, exotic scented inks of various colors, or multi-layered colored paper collages speckled with gold flecks, which can be used to create special effects. However, none of these effects will compensate for an unpracticed hand, and you should never forget that the greatest drama of Shodo is the simple struggle for space in black and white.

Certain conventions dictate the approximate placement of characters, columns, and *rakkan*, which are the seals, signature, and explanatory footnotes to the poem.

Fig. 9-2

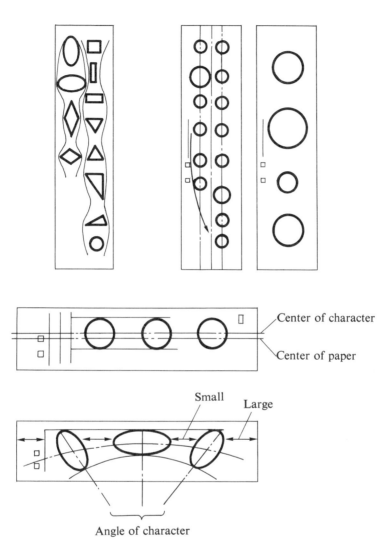

Center of character

Center of paper

Small   Large

Angle of character

In actual practice this is measured by eye, but general guidelines do exist for both rectangular *jôfuku* (Fig. 9-2) and square *shikishi* (Fig. 9-3). The actual placement depends on the composition, and may already be a part of the *tehon*. Since an exact copy is never possible, the student may need to make slight allowances in the placement of characters, considering the actual work, rather than relying strictly on theoretical principles. The placement of the seal (*inkan*) is considered very important, for this slight touch of red can help anchor the entire field of black.

You occasionally come across works which entirely violate all of the standards of mounting and display. A wild variation from the tried and true may be outstanding, but more likely not. In purchasing or displaying a work of calligraphy, first keep in mind the basic rules of composition, then try to judge the work on its other merits.

Fig. 9-3 *Shikishi*

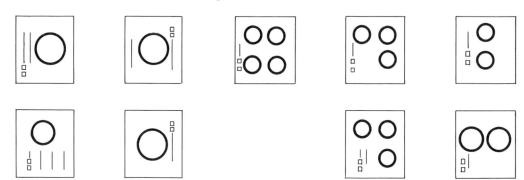

Provide Visual and Verbal Access to the Work

Fig. 9-4

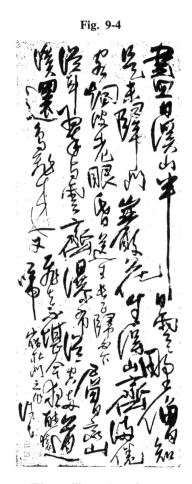

Calligraphy is originally a Chinese art. It is not surprising that most works display a Chinese phrase, proverb, or poem written entirely in *kanji*. The larger the number of characters, the more factors like style, composition and phrasing become important. A character with a particularly long stroke (*hamidashi*) may take a leading role. But this outstanding feature should enhance the other characters, not steal the stage (Fig. 9-4).

If the composition has only a few characters, and particularly if it features only one, then visual impact becomes more important than the meaning or style. It would seem easier to paint one or two large characters than several columns of small ones, but like a solo performer, the single character is all alone on stage. The fewer the characters, the more demanding the role each one has to play (Fig. 9-5).

There are also works in the purely Japanese script involving *hiragana* or *Man'yô-gana*. Some calligraphers work in *kana* alone, using such an archaic script that their work is completely illegible to the average Japanese untrained in calligraphy. Though the use of the brush is the same as for *kanji*, it is often more refined and delicate, using far less ink. The blotting effects of *nijimi* are rarely displayed in works of *kana*, and the dry effects of *kasure* are often stretched to the limit.

The calligraphy of *Man'yô-gana* is cultured and classical. Not only the writing style, but the subject matter itself is elegant and refined, written in the cadences of a distant era (Fig. 9-6). The emphasis is on the vertical line. Characters cascade in

Fig. 9-5

Fig. 9-6

Ro-yô Utagau Kan-gyoku o (A dewdrop
on a leaf, or is it a jewel?)

tall and thin streams, often connected together in long fluid strokes. The vertical
columns seem subject to a less formal discipline, like long strips of cloth given over
to the wind. The *Man'yô-gana* are actually *kanji*, which have been written in a
highly abbreviated *Sôsho* form. Used as a purely phonetic affixation, the meaning
of the original character is ignored. The script is so highly abbreviated that it bears
closer resemblance to the phonetic *hiragana* than to the *kanji* from which it came.
The *Man'yô-gana* are chosen from a limited selection of allowable forms, so that
the discipline of deciphering them is difficult, but not impossible. The fact that
a few bona fide *kanji* may also be included in the same poem leads to some confusion. The reader of the poem must not only be able to decipher the phonetic characters, but must be able to tell when they are being used for meaning and when
they are intended for pronunciation. Still, most classical poems are written almost
entirely in *kana*, and familiarity with the major prototypes simply means learning
to recognize a larger alphabet. In any case, the poem will probably require a caption for both meaning and pronunciation. These poems were originally meant to
be read aloud, although to fully appreciate the sound of the poetry requires a
knowledge of classical Japanese. Excellent translations are available for classical
Japanese poetry, but the Western calligrapher may have to consider this a rather
specialized branch of the art.

Haiku are concise three-line Japanese poems, which also enjoy a large following
in the West. Lesser known overseas, but equally popular in Japan are the five-line
poems known as *Tanka*, or short songs. *Haiku* are written in syllables of 5–7–5,

Fig. 9-7

Fig. 9-8

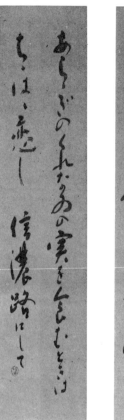

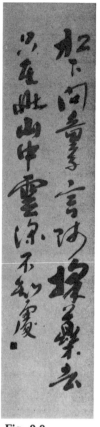

while *Tanka* are slightly longer with a 5–7–5–7–7 pattern. The Japanese language is well suited to these poetic forms, with its small number of vowels and a large number of short words. *Haiku* and *Tanka*, and even Western poetry in translation, are usually painted in a mixture of *kanji* and modern *hiragana* (Fig. 9-7). Original *Haiku* can be produced in English, but attempts to mimic the strict Japanese meter usually sound strained and fragmented. You can enjoy Japanese *Haiku* in translation, but calligraphy adds another dimension by giving you direct visual access to the poem. Still, the most popular form of calligraphy may be the Chinese poems written only in *kanji* (Fig. 9-8).

There is another style which seems to suit the modern mentality, which is avant-garde calligraphy. This is a frontier art, and few rules apply. Certainly legibility is not primary, and it remains for future generations to determine what value these abstract expressions in ink really have. It may be considered as calligraphy and not abstract art if some precedent can be found in the classics, whatever the style of the script (Fig. 9-9). However, there is no such thing as an untitled work in Shodo, because to qualify as calligraphy it must say something.

Fig. 9-9

Transfer the Brushwork to Other Media

There are several kinds of design applications which can be used to display calligraphy in non-traditional formats. But whatever the final medium of display, they all begin with the brush. Transferring a work to cloth by silkscreening methods produces a durable and handsome effect. A popular use of calligraphy on cloth is in the split half-curtains (*noren*) which beckon customers into Japanese shop entrances (Fig. 9-10).

Fig. 9-10

Fig. 9-11

Calligraphy makes a fitting decoration for pottery, and is often found on the tea cups which are used in Japanese restaurants (Fig. 9-11). Product labels such as those on Japanese *sake* bottles often display excellent original calligraphy, each reflecting the spirit of the product, or region in which it was made (Fig. 9-12). Japanese wine labels are very colorful, and make excellent collector's items, particularly if you are fond of the contents.

Letters carved in wood are known as *kokuji*. They may be carved into or out of the wood, and later painted to enhance or protect the surface (Fig. 9-13). Impressions carved out of soft alabaster can be used to make signature and art seals, known as *tenkoku*. The seal is pressed against a red colored putty-like substance (*in-niku*), and the raised portion of the seal produces a reversed impression on the paper. Depending on whether you carve out the figure or the ground, you can have red letters on a white field, or white letters on a red background (Fig. 9-14). Seals are conventionally used to sign or supplement a work of calligraphy, but *tenkoku* is also recognized as a separate branch of the art in itself.

Fig. 9-12

Fig. 9-13a　　　　　　Fig. 9-13b

Fig. 9-14

有
隣

The rewards of
goodness are close
at hand.

洗
心

Renew the mind.

Develop Original Ideas from Oriental Design

Even if you never pick up a brush, there are dozens of ways in which you can enjoy calligraphy, including travel, study, and design. The simplest pleasure is simply in looking, and the best place to look is in the countries where *kanji* are still in use. The Far East is the Mecca of calligraphy. Even when overseas travel is not a practical option, most large Western cities have Japan or China towns which maintain something of the flavor of the home country. Perhaps you have already been, but never noticed the wealth of brushwork all around you. When you know what to look

Fig. 9-15a　　　　　　Fig. 9-15b

Fig. 9-16

THE YOMIURI SHIMBUN

for, it opens up an entirely new world. Not all of it is good, but occasionally you find something superb. Excellent calligraphy is often carved in wood, or on the face of large boulders, which can be found in parks or temple grounds (Fig. 9-15). Calligraphy exhibits are commonplace in major Japanese cities, but it is also on display everywhere you look, on shop signs, menus, newspapers, calendars, and packages of every conceivable variety (Fig. 9-16).

Looking is free, but most people want something more tangible for their effort. High-quality photographic reproductions are available in books. You can easily purchase original works or reproductions at department stores and specialty shops. Calligraphy can give a contemporary Oriental accent to any Western interior, but it takes a trained eye to select quality. This is a field which is still virtually un-explored by Western collectors, investors, and interior designers.

You can also study calligraphy using reference materials found in libraries, museums, and galleries. Further resources, including personal instruction, may be available through colleges, foreign embassies, consulates, and cultural organiza-tions. You can have a certain amount of fun with a pencil or a brush-pen, but eventually you will want to work with a calligraphy brush and handmade paper. The proper materials can be ordered from an art supply or Oriental import store.

Use Calligraphy to Visualize and Magnify Thought

Shodo can also be enjoyed in a more introspective way: with philosophical sayings, mottos, or poetry for reflection and meditation. These can be displayed in your home or office, or printed on anything from a business card to a bookmark. There is a virtually inexhaustible range of themes and styles to fit any temperament. When well translated or rendered with a brush, Oriental proverbs can be a far cry from the cheap quips found in Chinese fortune cookies. A good classical Chinese poem can serve as inspiration for writing, philosophy, or meditation. In an indirect way, it can even stimulate your imagination for creative work in other media altogether, such as music, sculpture, or dance.

Rethinking the Western Interior

Many foreigners living in Tokyo have begun to find creative ways of decorating in a Japanese style, without completely living in it. In fact, few Japanese today live in an entirely traditional style. Most prefer a mixture of East and West, taking the best of each. An imaginative set of cross-cultural decorating ideas is presented in *Japanese Accents in Western Interiors* (by Peggy Landers Rao and Jean Mahoney, published by Shufunotomosha, Co., Ltd., Tokyo, 1988). Creative approaches include hanging sashes (*obi*) of *kimono* on the wall instead of wearing them, using antique Japanese doors for low table tops, or brightly labeled *sake* barrels for potted plants. Japanese antique shops sell a variety of objects which lend themselves to non-traditional uses.

Fig. 9-17a   **Fig. 9-17b**

But the use of calligraphy in design opens up an entirely new realm of possibilities. It lends itself well to other media like wood, ceramics, or cloth, as well as the more traditional display formats of the scroll and picture frame. Calligraphy can be displayed on the uneven surface of a Japanese folding fan (Fig. 9-17). Other possibilities include the open face fan and the folding screen. Decorating with Japanese cultural artifacts and antiques can be quite expensive, but calligraphy is something which you can produce yourself. You can even present it as a handmade gift, adapting it to the person, place, season or occasion.

Principles for Enjoying Calligraphy

To practice Shodo without ever performing or displaying your work would be like rehearsing a play without ever going on stage and showing it to an audience. Shodo is fundamentally a social art, an art of communication. Something charges the air when a work is put on display or performed live, under pressure. A successful work of art can focus and magnify the creative energy of its audience. Just as music is meant to be heard, calligraphy is meant to be seen.

Unfortunately, people on both sides of the language barrier often assume that non-native speakers of Chinese or Japanese are incapable of appreciating an art which they cannot read. The fault is not in their capacity to appreciate: it is in the fact that few people, including professional calligraphers themselves, take the trouble to give Westerners verbal or visual access to the art. The Japanese have a reputation for being very good at absorbing the best of foreign cultures, and very inept at exporting their own culture. A great deal of effort in both the Japanese private and public sectors is devoted to the export of products and technology, but comparatively little is being done to support the international understanding of Japanese culture and the arts. Japan today risks being seen overseas primarily as an economic competitor, with a technological genius and a workhorse mentality. If Western people could be shown how easy it is to enjoy and gain access to heretofore esoteric Japanese arts like Shodo, then they would come to recognize a more human Japanese face. The principles then, for learning to enjoy and appreciate calligraphy are:

1. **Respect the Conventions of Mounting and Display.**
2. **Provide Visual and Verbal Access to the Work.**
3. **Transfer the Brushwork to Other Media.**
4. **Develop Original Ideas from Oriental Design.**
5. **Use Calligraphy to Visualize and Magnify Thought.**

Chapter 10

The Character of Japanese Design

In Search of the Aesthetic Nucleus

The Japanese have a genius for reducing things to their functional and aesthetic essence, a gift for expressing the gist of a thing in visual terms. The products of this culture include many ingenious adaptations of foreign ideas, ranging from the folding fan to the automobile. These have been so appealing and so useful that they have captured the imaginations, and the markets of many foreign lands. A knowledge of the general principles of Japanese design will provide a base for understanding calligraphy in its cultural context.

It is important for an artist not to lose touch with the source of creativity. But artists who reject the collective, functional, or communicative needs of society risk being rejected themselves. At best, anti-social artists can expect a solitary struggle on the fringe. On the other hand, art which caters to political interests tends to be vulgar; while art which serves commercial interests risks mediocrity. Art and daily life do not always mix, nor should they be forced to. There is a place for the factory as well as the museum.

But in the world of design there is a union of function and beauty, and it is this world which the Japanese have so deftly mastered. Design is art in daily life. It is the visible evidence of communication between the conventional and the creative mind. A society which understands and supports its artists is likely to enjoy a renaissance of high culture and superb design in everything from fashion, to furniture, to interior living space. The Japanese have so long enjoyed this renaissance in their own culture, that at times they take it for granted. We can only hope that future generations will give it the same attention it has received in the past.

Bring the Far Near

Most people see the world as complex: obscure, illogical, precarious, puzzling, faraway. An exceptional few see it as simple: lucid, rational, secure, cherished, and close-at-hand. It is an enviable skill to be able to reduce the complexity of life to its simple essence, not only emotionally but physically. For to simplify something is to bring the far near, and to master it.

146

Fig. 10-1

There are many examples of this in Japanese culture, beginning with the art of food preparation and serving. Most Japanese food is designed to be served and consumed in bite-sized portions. Chopsticks are better at pinching a morsel of food than at cutting or dipping from a large mass of unportioned food. Meals often consist of small portions of a variety of dishes, served on delicate plates or in bowls of different shapes (Fig. 10-1). Sometimes the food is neatly packed in a box (*bentô*), or served on a tray, but always easy to take in single bites (Fig. 10-2). Preparation of the specialty food *sushi* uses nearly twenty steps to cut, season, and press a slice of raw fish onto a fingerful of rice to reduce it to a single mouthful (Fig. 10-3).

Fig. 10-2

Fig. 10-3

Many specialty restaurants exist in Japan, such as those serving raw fish (*sashimi*), deep-fried seafood and vegetables (*tempura*), noodles (*menrui*), charcoal broiled eel (*unagi*), light broth beef and vegetable stew (*sukiyaki*), and table stir-fried dishes (*teppanyaki*). Not only do many of these let you see the process of food preparation, but they often make a performance of it, or even let you do the easiest part for yourself. All of this brings the mysterious process of food preparation right before your eyes, ears, and finally your mouth.

Many symbols in Japan beckon the far near, and perhaps the most classical of these is the folding fan, or *sensu* (Fig. 10-4). The two most important parts of the fan are the *kaname*, or center from which the blades of the fan radiate, and the *sue-*

Fig. 10-4

hiro, or spread of the fan itself. The ribs of the fan can be outstretched to reveal the distant horizon, as in dance and theater, or drawn in to a compact unit that fits in the palm of the hand or rim of the sash. The fan is considered an auspicious sign because of the way it radiates out, and also a sign of authority because of the way it draws everything back to itself.

Fig. 10-5

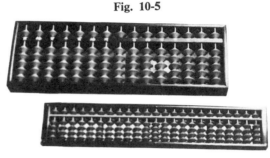

Another object which brings the far near is the abacus, or *soroban* (Fig. 10-5). Until recently commonly used in shops, restaurants, companies and even banks, the abacus reduces the complexity of calculation to a rapid and concise movement of wooden beads with the fingertips. For simple calculations, it is often as fast, and as accurate as a calculator. It probably even builds better calculating skills, because of the combined use of the fingertips, eyes, and simulaneous chanting of the voice, which to the uninitiated sounds like a Buddhist ceremony. There are even ranks of competence for the *soroban*, similar to the system used in the martial arts. A person skilled in the abacus can even manipulate it mentally, with no instrument in hand.

All of these objects have in common a skillful blend of elegance and utility. They bring the faraway near, and the universe home, giving us a sense of being able to live gracefully in the world.

Fig. 10-6a

Reveal the World within

Though the complex can be made simple, the ordinary can also be made elaborate. What better example than the art of *origami*, in which a simple square of paper can be transformed through a series of simple folds, to a bird, animal, flower, fish, mask, or complex geometric figure (Fig. 10-6). Beautifully colored and patterned paper can adorn these paper creations in the finest clothing. However, if the mind of the folder becomes con-

148

Fig. 10-6b

fused or distracted, the resulting piece will show it in lack of balance, symmetry, or grace. When the artist is fully relaxed, unhurried, and attentive, the folded creature seems to breathe life. We must not forget that the complex problems of the world often have simple solutions. But it is also true that the simplest and most unassuming things in life often contain an infinite range of possibilities.

Even in the art of gift wrapping, Japanese seem to prefer to wrap with a loose, flexible covering; which allows a glimpse of the world within rather than hermetically sealing it from without (Fig. 10-7). The Japanese have devised ingenious ways of wrapping boxes, bottles, flowers, and

Fig. 10-7

Fig. 10-8

Fig. 10-9

even money. A gift is considered to be an extension of the heart. It should be self-contained, but open to the outside. The same principles apply in the wearing of *kimono*, which involves wrapping oneself in clothing (Fig. 10-8); and in architecture, where rooms are only temporarily enclosed by sliding doors and translucent screens (Fig. 10-9).

149

Fig. 10-10

The Japanese intuitively sense that space is not empty or dimensionless. This explains their fascination with layering in organizations and products. The outside face never tells the whole story, not out of an effort to deceive, but out of a recognition that there is always more to a situation than it first appears. It is not only a shortage of space which led Japanese to create clever ways of storing objects. The concept of boxes-within-boxes is just one example of the cultural intuition that space is not merely empty, and that there are worlds within worlds (Fig. 10-10).

This is also evident in the art of masks. The *Noh* mask is the essence of the Japanese face, displaying little to the outside, but suggesting much of the world within (Fig. 10-11). The actor may

Fig. 10-11

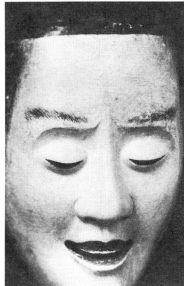

Fig. 10-12

hold a pose immovably for a long period of time, but imperceptible changes in the angle of the mask seem to disclose an ever changing cast of subtle emotions. Though Japanese dolls are often ornately costumed, they usually have very chaste facial expressions (Fig. 10-12). In Japan the face is not the place to display one's emotions.

The innocence of the simple exterior is easily misread. Often a courteous reception is only an invitation to a complex world within, a maze of interrelationships and possibilities that can overwhelm the unprepared. The beauty of simplicity is that it contains many possibilities. But the time comes when these must be consolidated in action. Just as the fan can be opened, so it can be closed. What could be more useful?

Unity of Calmness and Action

Living things are constantly in motion. One characteristic of many of the Japanese arts is the attempt to suspend motion, or at least slow it down. Hokusai's famous woodblock print provides a surging view of a giant wave, engulfing both men and mountain, yet leaving each intact (Fig. 10-13). There is great calmness at the eye of a hurricane. The most rapidly spinning top appears in a state of suspended animation. The Japanese artist recognizes that when motion is taken to the limit, it becomes very calm. The skill of the artist is in making this truth of nature plain to see.

Fig. 10-13

Fig. 10-14

The Japanese art of flower arranging (*ikebana*) captures the essence of the living flower through a simple spray of leaves and stems (Fig. 10-14). Seeing the flower's life in suspended motion, we become more aware of our own existence in nature. We too are cut off from nature, but through art are given back our identity. Life passes quickly, but art helps us notice it before it is gone.

Fig. 10-15a

Fig. 10-15b

The Japanese martial arts, from swordsmanship to Sumô, always begin in a posture of calmness (Fig. 10-15). The power of their motion springs from the silent source within, the unity of calmness and action. The martial artist whose feet dance around in an unsettled matter may be able to hypnotize or confuse a weaker person, but is no match for the one who can wait. The real struggle of the martial artist is not with his opponent: it lies in overcoming the divided self within.

Unity of Function and Beauty

The Japanese genius for design in manufacturing is well known. From electronics to umbrellas: new and more efficient products keep getting smaller, more compact, more beautiful. The ability to fuse function and beauty is nothing new in Japan. The family crest, usually displayed on the shoulder of a *kimono*, is far more concise and modern in appearance than its European equivalent (Fig. 10-16). Textile designs produced hundreds of years ago still strike us with the freshness of the hour (Fig. 10-17). Somehow the objects of daily life in Japan were never reduced to a rude functional simplicity, as they often were in other cultures, where lack of money often meant lack of decoration.

Pottery is a very functional art, originally providing the daily utensils of food

Fig. 10-16

Fig. 10-17b

Fig. 10-17a

and drink. The indigenous forms of pottery in Japan show the same attention to beauty in the service of function (Fig. 10-18). From the irregular shape to the uneven glaze, everything shuns sameness. The potter seeks individual expression through endless aesthetic variations on limited functional themes.

Fig. 10-18

Expressing the Universal in the Particular

The Universe is an undivided whole; a vast interconnected web of mass and energy. Though the Universe is vast, it is mirrored everywhere in the microcosm of its parts. We may know this intellectually, but can it be expressed visually through design?

The art of Japanese joinery (*kigumi*) is one in which wooden beams are interlocked and assembled without nails (Fig. 10-19). The effect is both physically stable and aesthetically pleasing. Wooden beams constructed in this way work themselves into true during an earthquake, and actually strengthen the building's resistance to the tremors. A miniature version of this art is found in the construction of wooden puzzles. The pieces are so tightly interlocked that it seems almost impossible to break inside, until at last you move the

Fig. 10-19

Fig. 10-20

appropriate piece, and gradually figure out how to take it apart (Fig. 10-20). The whole is expressed through the interlocking of the parts.

A two dimensional variation of this is found in a puzzle known variously as the Lucky Puzzle, Board of Wisdom, or Tangrams. A rectangular board is sectioned into seven unequal geometric shapes, which can be combined to produce a hundred or more distinct silhouettes (Fig. 10-21). This puzzle is such a challenge to the

Fig. 10-21

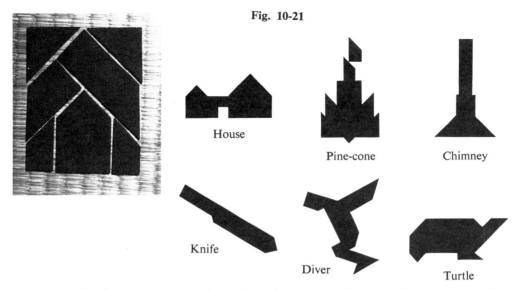

House

Pine-cone

Chimney

Knife

Diver

Turtle

visual imagination, that many schools have incorporated it into their science and mathematics programs.

Many Japanese enjoy studying *Tsume-Go*, an abbreviated form of the board game of *Go*, in which white and black stones are placed on the intersecting points of the board's cross-grid, in an effort to surround and capture territory. *Tsume-Go* involves short, tactical problems, which can be solved in a few minutes, while the actual game may take several hours to play (Fig. 10-22). These *Go* problems are reduced to the barest simplicity, so that one or two moves can secure, or lose the entire group of stones. The positions and interactions of the pieces are so tightly bound as to be measured in the integrity of each move. Many who play the game feel that the same thing is true in life as well.

Fig. 10-22

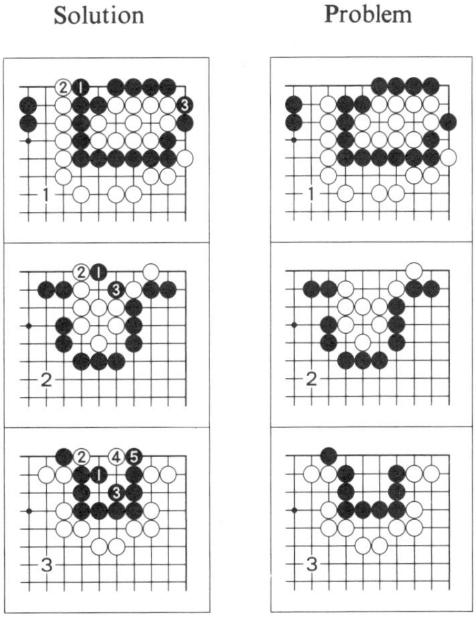

Solution   Problem

The World on Paper

Each of these design principles has influenced the Japanese arts, and calligraphy itself has had a major influence on Japanese design. The Way of the Brush encompasses an entire universe of culture, character, and individual life experience. Many poems written in calligraphy express the essence of life in poetry or philosophy. What you put on paper is a culmination of all that went before. Many design

154

discoveries were made by people actively engaged in study of one of the arts. Creativity is more than an intellectual exercise. Ideas are born when the hands work in cooperation with the eyes and the brain.

The world of design is touched by calligraphy in another way, through the use of lettering. There are entire scripts that have been invented for, or adopted by certain professions as a kind of trademark, which reveals yet another face of *kanji*. The actors of *Kabuki* use a flamboyant script which is consistent with their extravagent costumes and style (Fig. 10-23). The names of *Sumô* wrestlers competing in a tournament are always depicted in a unique script, which calls their massive and immovable forms to mind (Fig. 10-24). This use of lettering is like a talisman, a seal of faith that the professional will perform in character. The

Fig. 10-23

Kabuki script: Edo period (left) and modern (right)

Fig. 10-24

Sumô script: Edo period (left) and modern (right)

Fig. 10-25

Rakugo script

Fig. 10-26

Rakugo storyteller uses a special type of lettering to advertise his trade, which reflects the way in which he fills every moment with lively, non-stop monologue, expressive gestures and energetic pantomime (Fig. 10-25). The script leaves very little white space. This calls to mind the way the storyteller fills our ears, as well as the auditorium, to the brim.

Specialty restaurants sometimes take advantage of a particular feature of their cuisine, and design it into the lettering of the shop sign or menu. A shop specializing in deep-fried foods served on bamboo skewers uses long strokes with pointed tips in the lettering of their shop insignia (Fig. 10-26). An eel shop (*unagi*) writes the *hiragana* for "*u*" on their shop curtain so that it resembles an eel, head and all (Fig. 10-27). These kinds of variations in script are made possible by the visual imagery of the *kanji* and the versatility of the brush.

Fig. 10-27

Principles of Design in Japanese Culture

Language is the verbal aspect of culture. But the language of calligraphy has a visual dimension as well. The art does not exist in isolation, but in the context of the culture as a whole. We can see the influence of the brush on nearly all aspects of Japanese art, language, and design. For their own part, the Japanese have their eyes firmly fixed on the West, attempting to learn and adapt the best of all that they see. Why can we not do the same? We need not imitate or try to become Japanese to learn from their unique vision of the world, which is at once practical and artistic. The principles by which the Japanese design their world are:

1. **Bring the Far Near.**
2. **Reveal the World within.**
3. **Find the Unity of Calmness and Action.**
4. **Seek the Unity of Function and Beauty.**
5. **Express the Universal in the Particular.**

Chapter **11**:

Reading between the Lines

Handwriting East and West

Rudyard Kipling was not the first to feel the enormous chasm that separates East and West. Perhaps nowhere are cultural differences so clearly reflected as in language. No two systems could be any more different those using pictorial *kanji* and those employing a phonetic romanized alphabet. Scientists have identified different parts of the brain which are specialized for various language functions, such as the production of speech, writing, naming colors, reading, or naming objects (Fig. 11-1 a and b). People suffering localized brain damage have been known to recognize, but not be able to repeat speech. Similarly, a brain damaged person may be able to read a pictographic script, but not a phonetic one. Ordinarily, all parts of the brain work in concert to recognize and reproduce language. Nevertheless, it has been clearly established that different parts of the brain specialize in different language functions.

There are several major things which separate a pictographic script from a phonetic one. Characters are complex and numerous, alphabetic symbols are simple and few in number. Characters are pictorial or ideo-graphic, while the alphabet is phonetic. *Kanji* were designed to be written vertically in columns, from top right to bottom left, while languages using the Roman alphabet are written horizontally in rows, from top left to bottom right. Eye movements reflect brain activity, and the

Fig. 11-1a	**Fig. 11-1b**

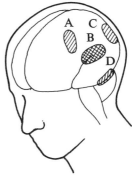

A—Speech production
B—Speech comprehension
C—Connections allowing
    spontaneous response

A—Writing
B—Naming colors
C—Reading
D—Naming

brain is stimulated as the hand produces and the eye follows writing. Though perhaps an oversimplification, vertical eye movements are tied to the visual imagination, while horizontal eye movements are more a function of the auditory imagination. When trying to recall a face, people often look up toward the ceiling; when trying to recall a name, they more often look off to the side.

But perhaps more important still are the differences which arise from a writing system designed for the brush, and one designed for the hard-tipped pen. If the brush had not been invented or used as a writing tool, Oriental thought might have developed along totally different lines. Unfortunately, few non-calligraphers have much occasion to use a brush anymore in modern Japan. Westernization may have made it easier for the Japanese to conduct business in the modern world, but it has also cost them dearly in loss of cultural identity and traditional values.

As great as the differences are, we should be careful not to overlook the similarities. Japanese also use phonetic alphabets, *kana* and *romaji*, to supplement their primary use of characters. The business of daily life is more often than not conducted in non-cursive, horizontal writing or printing, just as in the West. Eye-hand-brain coordination functions in much the same way in both systems of handwriting. Both are learned skills, which depend greatly on habit and training. Both reflect the mental and physical condition of the author through the same unconscious processes. In either case, handwriting can be improved or changed through conscious awareness and practice.

Both use conventional symbols which are legible to the educated public. While children in both countries learn a standard form of penmanship, few people maintain that style into adulthood. Differences in adult handwriting reflect differences in personality, and it is very difficult in either case to forge another person's writing. Despite the surface differences between the two systems of writing, the brain that comprehends them is much the same underneath.

The analysis of handwriting is both an art and a science. Not all experts agree on the meaning of particular points, but it is reliable enough for policework. Both government and private business in Europe use handwriting analysis as part of the hiring process. And while it is no magic key to the unconscious, handwriting can provide important clues when used in combination with common sense, historical data, and intuitive awareness. Some features of handwriting reflect integral and desirable aspects of a person's personality, but not all. Signs of stress, and mental or physical illness appear in handwriting, and are certainly worth correcting. These are signs of distress, not prognosis of disease, but like a slip of the tongue, they can reveal that which is ordinarily kept from view. A steady hand reflects a steady mind and a sound body.

Handwriting analysis in the wrong hands can deteriorate into a cheap form of fortune-telling. A cheap analysis is characterized by two things: formula thinking and a deterministic philosophy. The formula thinker does not look at the person, but relies on charts and formulas to calculate the personality stereotype, and usually offers you a diagnosis without a prescription. The implication is that you must learn to live with the way you are. Thinking in stereotypes is an easy way to avoid facing particulars.

How then do you learn to recognize the real thing? Experience with the brush

158

gives you the accuracy of perception that is required for making good judgments of handwriting. What does the calligrapher see that may elude even the author of the handwritten text? Calligraphy combines the talents of the forger with the originality of the painter. The artist in any medium develops a sensitivity to it which seems like magic to the average person. In the same way the calligrapher develops a sensitivity to the handwritten line. Many of the principles which apply to the brush also apply to the pen. Once you understand how to read between the lines in *kanji*, you can begin to apply this knowledge to our own writing as well.

Maintain a Generous Sense of Internal Space

Fig. 11-2

One of the first characters which a Japanese child learns to draw is the word for mouth, a simple square. Children are taught to connect all of the corners of the square (*seppitsu*), as it appears in print. However, many adults do not connect the first and second strokes, leaving the upper left hand corner open (Fig. 11-2). Either way of connecting strokes is perfectly legible. However the person is rarely conscious of which way he is writing until it is pointed out.

What subconscious impulse makes a person want to leave open, rather than seal off the connecting strokes in a character? The box is the basic unit of the houses that we live in. It contains us and protects our belongings from the forces of the environment. Once survival needs are met, human beings begin to develop ways of opening up that box to the outside world. It would be intolerable to live in an enclosed space without windows or doors. The window is a statement of one's relationship to society. The cultured person remains open to external ideas and influences, while the person who bars the world out lives in a prison of his own making. Even so, the world is a dangerous place. It would be extremely foolish to never close your doors or windows. Freedom is the ability to choose and vary one's relationships to the world.

Fig. 11-3

Closed

Open

Indefinite

In most masterworks of calligraphy, you will find some connected strokes open and some closed, but all well defined. It is considered acceptable to join or separate connected strokes, as long as you make it clear which you have chosen (Fig. 11-3). It is important to show that the stroke was placed with purpose and control. A stroke which touches but does not engage is considered weak and indecisive.

Success in business depends on knowing when to delegate and when to maintain firm control. Management requires

Fig. 11-4

Retains.

Releases.

flexibility. Dealing with every situation in the same way will eventually lead to loss of control. Neither the bohemian nor the tightfisted can manage or invest money well. You need to accumulate money in order to be able to invest it later. The psychology of this can be expressed visually in a person's handwriting (Fig. 11-4). Think of the character as a visual container into which fluid is poured from the top. In one case the fluid is contained or redirected to other containers in the lower parts of the character, and little is lost. In the other case most of the liquid leaks out through the many openings in the character. If all of the corners of the connected strokes were tightly sealed then nothing could enter in the first place. Writing the character in the proper way conditions your subconscious mind to be alert to when to give, when to spend, and when to retain.

Fig. 11-5

Is it desirable to accumulate as much money as possible? Many of the very rich are also very neurotic, their lives spoiled by greed and mistrust. On the other hand, without a capacity to accumulate money, you lose many opportunities to develop yourself, make others happy, or contribute to society. The capacity to accumulate money is indicated in handwriting by a generous space between the left and right hand radicals of the character, known as the *futokoro*, or vest pockets of the character (Fig. 11-5). If the *futokoro* is big, it indicates a generous capacity to accumulate and use money. If it is narrow, it may indicate a self-limiting tendency. If your characters have a tight *futokoro*, this can be corrected by making a conscious effort to leave more space between the radicals.

There may seem to be no immediate connection between the writing of a character and the world of business. But many of the leaders in Japan's business and financial world exhibit this feature in their handwriting (Fig. 11-6). In both business and handwriting, behavior tends to be influenced by unconscious habit. There is often a striking similarity between the way that a person drives, eats, takes risks, or conducts business. All of these behaviors are cut from the same cloth. Our behavior reveals us to the world, and to the extent that we control it, we can influence our future. We do not need to have our fortunes told. We tell them every day in the way that we think, talk, and act.

Fig. 11-6

1. Otsuka Masashi, consultant to Otsuka Pharmaceuticals
2. Murai Tsutomu, president of Asahi Beer
3. Tashiro Kikuo, president of Asahi Television
4. Tabuchi Setsuya, president of Nomura Securities
5. Kamei Masao, president of Sumitomo Electrical Engineering
6. Tokuma Sumao, president of Sumitomo Marine and Fire Insurance
7. Mori Kazuo, president of Tôyô Suisan
8. Arai Masa-aki, president of Sumitomo Life Insurance
9. Hinokiyama Hiroshi, former president of Marubeni
10. Abekawa Sumio, president of Daiwa Bank
11. Takei Hirotomo, president of Chisan
12. O-ki Kôshirô, consultant to Saitama Bank
13. Kitsuda Yoshikazu, director of Nomura Securities
14. Kamisaka Kôya, president of Kinki Sôgô Bank
15. Tatsumi Keigo, vice president of Tôyô Information Systems

Maintain Regular Intervals between Horizontal Strokes

One thing that separates civilized from primitive man is skill in the orderly organization of intervals. We see it everywhere in society: people, data, and things spaced at regular intervals. Without a sense for the importance of intervals, cars could not proceed in traffic, buildings could not be built, books could not be printed. We would have neither music, gardens, nor parks. Parallel lines are a nearly certain sign of human habitation.

Characters in calligraphy are painted in a confined space, with the strokes placed at roughly equal intervals. The parallel spacing of horizontal strokes at equal intervals is known as *tôkankaku* (Fig. 11-7). This quality gives the character internal strength. It is a visible reflection of your own spatial awareness and unbroken concentration. This feature in handwriting correlates very closely with high scores on Japanese intelligence tests, good marks in school, and efficient work procedures in an office environment (Fig. 11-8). Carelessness usually results in lack of *tôkankaku*; and it is not surprising that this too would be reflected in work habits.

Fig. 11-7

Fig. 11-8

Irregular intervals	Regular intervals

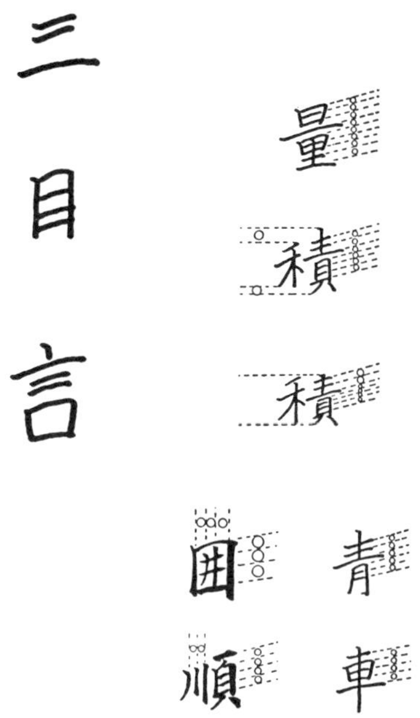

Fig. 11-9

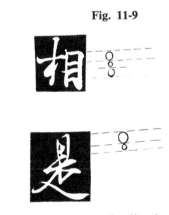

But perfect order is too austere. The point is control, not standardization. Still, only one who has mastered *tôkankaku* can deviate from it with impunity. O-gishi often broke the monotony of regularly spaced strokes deliberately, to very good effect (Fig. 11-9). If this were the rule, rather than the exception, we would have chaos. The break in the rhythm is unexpected, and therefore all the more effective. Partly because events in daily life are so predictable, we show great interest when they take a dramatic turn.

Maintain Good Attitude in Your Written Characters

A person's attitude is faithfully reflected in his bearing. The way you carry yourself is the visible aspect of your mental disposition. In Japanese the same characters are used to write the words posture and attitude (*shisei*). The most obvious manifestation of *shisei* in the written character is its orientation, its emphasis on the vertical or the horizontal. The same character may be written tall and thin (*tate-nagai*) or short and wide (*hira-tai*), as shown in Fig. 11-10.

Fig. 11-10

The attitude of the written character is an expression of the author's basic orientation. Active types prefer a horizontal orientation, which is directed away from the self, toward the outside world. Reflective personalities prefer the vertical orientation, which points like the needle of a compass toward the self. This orientation has nothing to do with being self-centered or egotistical. It refers to the priority placed on the sequence of thought and action. Reflective types prefer to think first and act later, active types act first and think afterward. Reflective types are calmer, take their time, and tend to be more refined. But active types are more outgoing, dynamic, and capable of taking care of business. The best approach adopts some qualities of each according to the situation.

Fig. 11-11

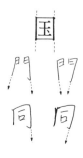

What happens when one attitude is preferred to the exclusion of the other? An unbalanced preference for reflection may lead to laziness or procrastination; while a hyperactive person tends to jump to conclusions, make mistakes, treat things and people too casually. A mature person can be comfortable with either one, even while showing a clear preference for one or the other. The work of the master calligraphers is rich in both.

A good attitude is one which is balanced and adaptable. Not only does it contain a variety of orientations in the text, but the base of each character is wide and stable (Fig. 11-11). It has the *suehiro* quality of the folding fan, radiating out from the apex. A wide base is considered an auspicious sign, like the national symbol of Mt. Fuji, or the gates to the Shinto shrines (Fig. 11-12). A narrow base appearing too frequently in a person's handwriting may be a sign of instability. If this feature appears in the handwriting of the chief executive of a Japanese firm, it may reflect badly on the company's prospects (Fig. 11-13).

Fig. 11-12   Fig. 11-13

Avoid the Collapse of Enclosed Spaces

A person under stress tends to apply more pressure in handwriting, and may tend to bear down on other things and people as well. This can lead to exhaustion, because a tremendous amount of energy is wasted in useless tension. Signs of this stress appear quite early in the form of collapsed internal spaces (*kûkan-no-tsubure*), in both Japanese and English handwriting (Fig. 11-14). A lapse of attention due to fatigue may be so brief that it goes by unnoticed, yet it leaves a physical trace in the handwriting. As small as it is, it is nevertheless a real sign of distress. Doctors claim that the majority of modern illnesses are stress induced, and preventable if detected early. The collapse of internal spaces in handwriting is a sign of stress, not a sympton of disease. Taking care to preserve these spaces is a good way to begin taking responsibility for your own health.

Fig. 11-14

A person whose posture is habitually slumped is putting undue stress on the internal organs and nerves of the body. This can weaken the life-force and lead to a breakdown of the immunity system. Poor posture usually results in shallow or labored breathing, preventing vital oxygen from reaching the tissues. Poor circulation fails to remove the toxins and waste products of metabolism, and can cause untold health problems. The posture, relaxation, and breathing required in using the brush all help to counteract these bad habits; which may be the reason why the ancient Chinese felt that calligraphy could prolong life. You simply cannot paint good calligraphy in a bad posture.

The brush strokes surround the internal spaces of the character like a rib cage surrounding a living lung. These parts seem to breathe when the *shisei* of the character is good. Improperly crossed strokes, excessive pressure, and tight writing patterns are all reflections of tension in the hips, neck, and shoulders. This tension is communicated directly to the brush through the arm and fingertips. The brush is so sensitive that it picks up any trace of useless tension and magnifies it into an ugly form. The difficulty of painting characters may produce its own tension, so to paint correctly, you must learn to relax under pressure. Tension frustrates human relationships and can ruin your health. Relaxation is your best natural immunity against disease.

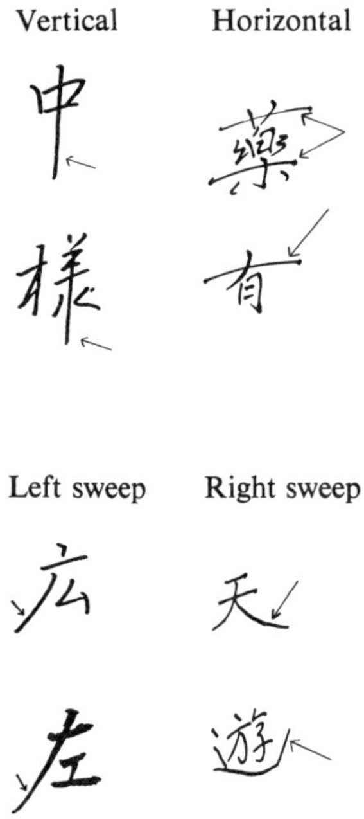

In type-set printing, all characters are of equal size. They are standardized to fit into columns of print which are easy to read. Ruled paper for hand-written reports is known as *genkô-yôshi*. The paper is ruled into rows or columns of boxes. Each character is confined by the ruled lines of the paper.

The rules of society exert a powerful restraining influence on behavior. In Japan, the educational

Fig. 11-15

Fig. 11-16 *Types of Hamidashi*

Vertical   Horizontal

Left sweep   Right sweep

system is highly standardized in an effort to preserve this rigid order. Fortunately, the human soul is not so easily dominated. In handwriting, the desire for freedom of expression is reflected in the way in which certain strokes break out of the real or imagined lines of the paper (*hamidashi*). In all but the most formal handwriting, people frequently go out of the lines (Fig. 11-15).

There are several types of *hamidashi*, each of which reflects a different type of vital energy (Fig. 11-16). Horizontal strokes, written from left to right, are comparatively short in most characters. A short stroke represents conservation of energy, while a long one represents a release of it. Horizontal *hamidashi* are a sign of productive energy or organizational intelligence. There are more horizontal strokes than vertical ones in most characters, but the vertical stroke tends to run through and unify the character, like a backbone supporting its center. Vertical *hamidashi* represent an energy of self-assertion and individuality. A very long vertical stroke suggests an independent spirit or unique character. This is a good thing if it appears once in a while, but if this line asserts itself too often, we may find ourselves faced with a stubborn egotist. The stroke may also break out in diagonal sweeps to the lower left or right. Left diagonals preceed right ones in the stroke order, and relate respectively to the energies of carrying on and following through.

Short straight strokes represent energy which is restrained, conserved, or analytically applied. Long curved lines reflect energy which is more emotional and freely expressed. Obviously, no one can say which is better, for it depends on preference and personality. A particular style of *hamidashi* may or may not fit you, but writing it gives you a chance to see how it feels. Practicing the various types of *hamidashi* which appear in the classics can expand your appreciation for a range of personality types, and may increase your own expressive repertoire in the process (Fig. 11-17).

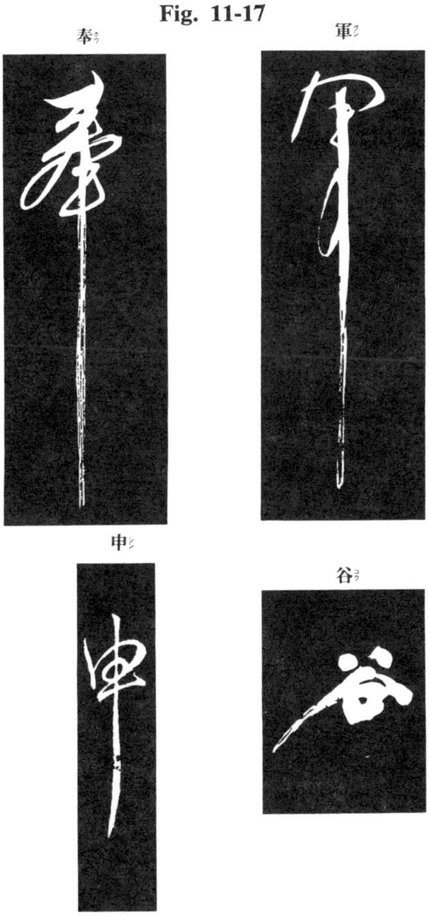

What does it mean if a person's handwriting exhibits no *hamidashi* whatsoever (Fig. 11-18)? It may mean a perfectly average personality, with no outstanding or extreme qualities. It may reflect a degree of contentment with the status quo, or even a condition of self-satisfaction. It probably also means that the person is responsible enough to follow the rules, but may lack the imagination to see beyond them.

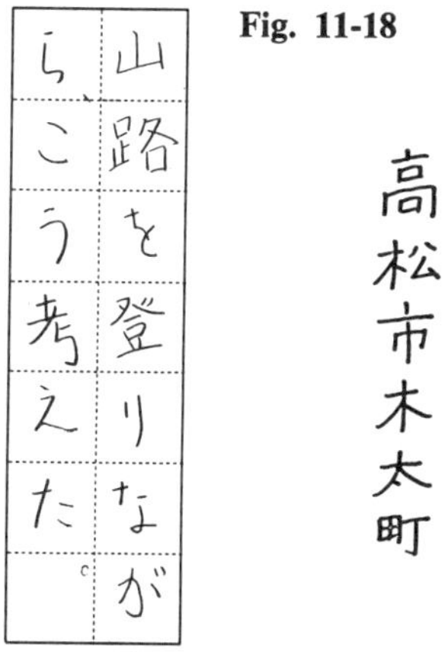

Fig. 11-17

奉　軍
申　谷

Fig. 11-18

山路を登りながら
こうこう考えた

高松市木太町

There is nothing wrong with staying within the lines, there are times when it is necessary. But there is also a danger in making a cut of the commonplace. Too much standardization tends to reject anything that is different, and may try to crush qualities of excellence when they appear. Obviously there are limits to freedom. The unrestrained exercise of appetite, passion, or inspiration leads straight to chaos. We need business-as-usual most of the time, but if they is all that we get, we are no better than machines.

Keep the Clarity of the Line Unbroken

While the spatial orientation of the characters tells us about a person's attitude, the rhythm of the vertical column tells us more about the sense of time. In attempting to hold the vertical line, the calligrapher is basically steering toward a target. It takes great concentration and steadiness to maintain a straight line, which is why this type of writing is often found among people who are trained in strict traditional disciplines (Fig. 11-19). More often the characters seem to weave back and forth. If the vertical weave is smooth and graceful, the person who wrote it probably has a good sense of rhythm. If the line is jagged, it indicates a tendency to react, rather than lead (Fig. 11-20). The adjustments in the line are more or less automatic, more a matter of what feels right than of any deliberate calculation. The writer's sense of rhythm is also expressed by the intervals left between the characters (Fig. 11-21). A busy or impatient person will tend to crowd the characters

Fig. 11-19

Fig. 11-20

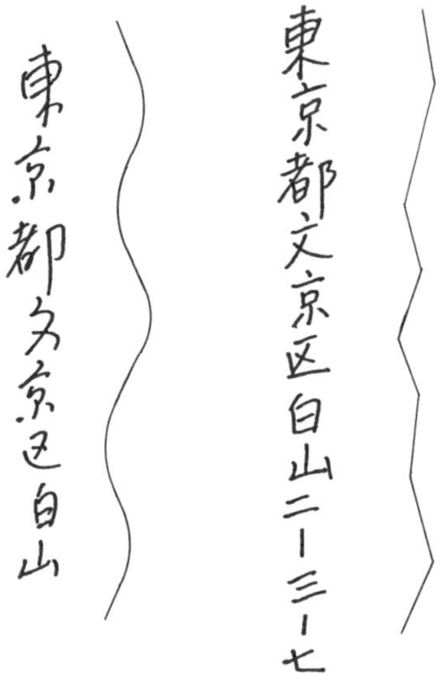

Fig. 11-21

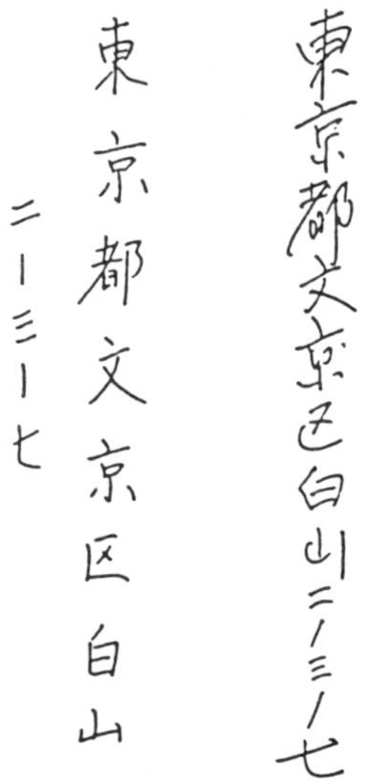

Fig. 11-22   **Fig. 11-23**

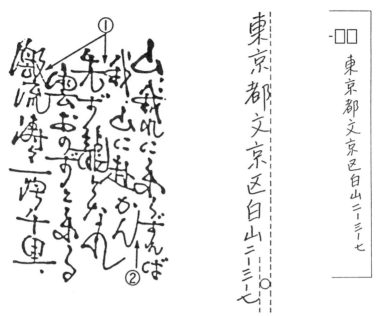

together, like a car tailgating in traffic. The easygoing writer will prefer to leave lots of space in between. An adaptable person uses flexible spacing, taking into account the edges of the paper and the columns to either side. A person who is accident prone, or lives dangerously, may write columns which carelessly overlap each other (Fig. 11-22). The intervals with which we choose to space our letters tell a lot about the way we conduct our lives.

Though you may try to write in straight columns, there are no guidelines on unruled paper. In addressing a post card, it is very easy to drift to one side or the other without noticing the shift in the column (Fig. 11-23). A gradual drift to the left, or center of the page, indicates a desire to move forward, and reflects an optimistic temperament. A drift back toward the right edge is a sign of withdrawal, or holding back. An extroverted personality will prefer to fill the space or dominate the center, like a puppy run loose. A more reserved personality will prefer to stay closer to the edges, observing things like a cat (Fig. 11-24). The amount of space that a person leaves at the top and bottom of the page is also significant (Fig. 11-25). When the characters are squeezed at the bottom, it may reflect a tendency to begin working harder with the approach of a deadline. Leaving ample space at the bottom by choosing to start a new column may reflect a desire to get things done well ahead of time.

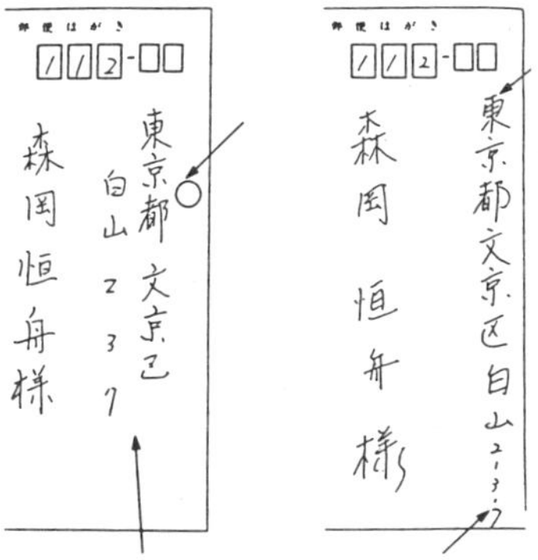

Even changes in the size of the characters give a clue to the writer's sense of

Fig. 11-24

rhythm. A good balance of large and small characters indicates aesthetic sensitivity, but also says something about attitudes toward other people in society. Does the writer allow for a wide range of types in his social and business life, or does he limit himself to those who have the same values and opinions? Are others ignored, or are their needs taken into account? The one thing that we all have in common is that we are all different. To value and encourage those differences is to expand your capacity as an artist and as a human being.

Fig. 11-25

Do Not Leave Fortune up to Chance

Anthropologist Margaret Meade calls personal responsibility our most important evolution, and the idea that we are a product of our environment our greatest sin. Our problems begin when we rely too heavily on others to forecast the future that we ourselves should be busy creating. To live life to the fullest, we must do so as actor, not as reactor. The exercise of this choice is what makes us human. You can take responsibility to make things happen, or you can let things happen to you, and blame other people and circumstances for your fate. Adaptability is not the absence of goals, but the presence of options.

Fig. 11-26

Fortune-telling, the attempt to read the course of future events from signs and symbols, is as old as humanity itself, and just as fallible. Nothing in life comes with a set of instructions, though often the truth is plain to see. One of the earliest methods of Chinese fortune-telling involved the etching of magic inscriptions, probably primitive characters, into soft tortoise shells, which were then heated until they cracked (Fig. 11-26). Astrologers would then attempt to read Heaven's advice from the pattern of the cracks, and on which side the characters fell.

The problem with this is that it relies on an arbitary interpretation of a random physical occurence. In the ancient East as well as the West, the bearer of bad news was often put to death, so early astrologers developed the art of casting only favorable, or very dubious horoscopes, in an effort to ensure their own survival.

One might be tempted to group handwriting analysis in the same category. But handwriting is a direct physical and mental trace of the person. It is unique, like a fingerprint, and very difficult for another person to copy. With practice, one might be able to learn to forge a signature, but not well enough to fool an expert. Even if you manage to copy a few lines well, there is a subconscious resistance to writing in a style other than your own, which will make itself known the moment that you let down your guard. Handwriting is an unconscious habit, which reflects the mental and physical condition of its author. It helps you take the pulse of the psyche.

Fig. 11-27

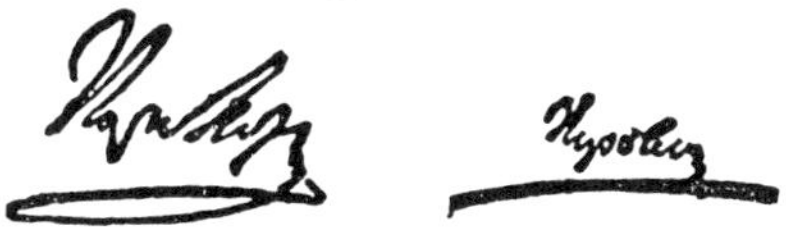

Fig. 11-28

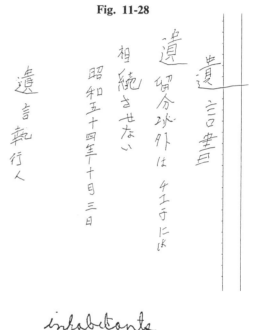

Handwriting changes with age and mood. Napoleon's signature before and after his defeat at Waterloo are a dramatic illustration of this (Fig. 11-27). Mental and physical illnesses both appear in a person's handwriting, often long before they become obvious enough to diagnose (Fig. 11-28). The pen is like a psycho-physical seismograph, registering the delicate connection between eye, hand, and brain. The handwritten line amplifies and makes visible subconscious tremors that might otherwise go undetected. Certainly good penmanship alone is no insurance against mental or physical adversity. But certain aspects of a person's writing are significant.

Penmanship is something that all children learn in school, and most childrens' handwriting is quite similar. Slight differences in early habits develop into adult handwriting which is often as unique as a signature. If bad writing habits exceed the bounds of legibility and aesthetics, we may think of trying to improve our handwriting. There is no need to go back to the models we learned early in life. Good handwriting preserves the unique style of the individual, but it also reflects a healthy attitude. The important question is what effect does an improvement in handwriting have on the rest of one's life? If these changes lead to a gradual improvement in one's health, personality, and performance, then they are worth the effort it takes. These few common criteria can help you preserve and express your unique style, while ensuring that you are developing in a positive way.

Principles of Auspicious Handwriting

The word "quick" once meant alive, the opposite of dead. In Shodo as well, the life of the strokes is measured in the speed and coordination of their execution. Movements of the brush should be youthful, fast, and clean. Fast writing is a sign of intelligence, a trace of rapid thought. Learn to move freely, without friction or hesitation. Watch the movements of dancers, atheletes, even animals and children. Nerve, muscle, and organ tissues are revitalized by proper use, but they atrophy and decay with inactivity. Premature senility may result from settling too quickly into a sedentary life. Walking is the best exercise of all: rhythmic, free of strain, involving the whole body, and costing nothing. A brisk walk can build your appetite for Shodo, for it builds a sense of rhythm, frees the mind, and oxygenates the blood.

Strengthen your life-force through the brush by learning to coordinate mind and body. Learn to walk and write with confidence. Place your strokes with purpose and mastery, and your future will surely be bright. The principles for auspicious handwriting are:

1. **Preserve a Generous Sense of Internal Space.**
2. **Respect the Regular Intervals between the Strokes.**
3. **Maintain Good Attitude in Your Written Characters.**
4. **Avoid Collapse of Enclosed Spaces.**
5. **Keep the Clarity of the Line Unbroken.**

Chapter 12

A Gallery of Works

Calligraphy and Translations by the Author.

Jôfuku are first painted on long rectangular paper, and then mounted on a scroll for permanent display. Calligraphy is best appreciated when you can stand before it face to face, so it is usually hung in a prominent and uncluttered place. Whether the subject is poetic or philosophical, *Jôfuku* is designed to lift the mind above daily concerns, through a sustained and concentrated outpouring of the spirit. Like a feature film with many intricate subplots, it unrolls a story over time. *Jôfuku* are considered closest to the essence of the art of calligraphy.

 Shikishi, on the other hand, are more like an action photograph; painted in a short burst of energy, and designed to give the viewer an instant impression. Painted on thick premounted paper, they can be framed or attached to a wall hanging. Many short Chinese and Japanese sayings lend themselves to the smaller size of the paper. *Shikishi* are often given as gifts to commemorate new beginnings: marriage, birth, entering a new job or school, or starting a new business. Because they are usually written for the occasion or people involved, their value is often more personal than artistic.

Jôfuku

Fig. 12-1

1. Rei-dan Ji-chi
You must experience hot and cold to know it.
A Zen expression meaning that Life is a direct encounter which cannot be explained in words.

Fig. 12-2

2. Tenchi Ujô
The Universe has Heart.
An expression by the famous novelist, Natsume Sôseki, meaning that the Universe is not a chaotic or haphazard place; and that Life is rich with purpose, emotion, and meaning.

3. *Sashô Hi ni Kyôjite Bansen o Tsuiyasu. Nomu koto, Chôgei no Hyakusen o Sû ga Gotoshi.*
Sashô spends a fortune on his daily pleasures.
He drinks like a whale inhaling a hundred rivers.
> —Toho, *Song of Eight Druken Sages*

Fig. 12-3

Fig. 12-4

4. *Ureuru Nakare Zenro Chiki Naki o, Tenka Tare Bitoka Kimi o Shirazaru.*
Feeling your apprehension knowing nothing of the road ahead, and no one knowing you.
> —Kôteki, Tang Poet

Words of encouragement to a friend embarking on a voyage to an unknown land.

174

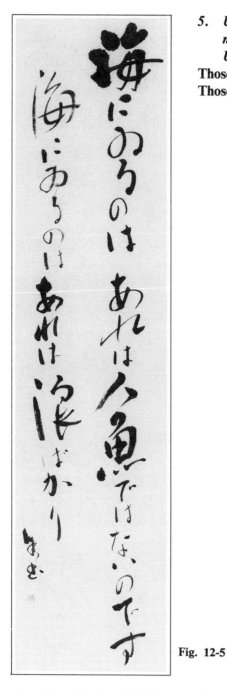

Fig. 12-5

5. *Umi ni iru no wa, Are wa Ningyo de wa nai no desu.*
Umi ni iru no wa, Are wa Nami bakari.
Those are not mermaids that we see,
Those are only waves.

—Nakahara Chûya, *The Northern Sea*

Fig. 12-6

6. *Take Fukaku, Ki Mitsu ni shite, Mushi no naku tokoro, Toki ni Biryô aru mo, Kore Kaze narazu.*
Deep in the Bamboo thicket, where the air is cool and the insects sing,
Here, the Wind cannot find us.

—Yôbanri, *Seeking Coolness on a Summer Night*

7. *Wa Ki, Shô o Itasu.*
The softening of extremes is an auspicious sign.

—Kanjo

In politics or in health, perhaps this is what is meant by the balance of *yin* and *yang*.

Fig. 12-7

Fig. 12-8

8. *Rihaku Itto*
Shihyaku hen,
Chôan-shi Jôshuka ni nemuru.
Tenshi yobi kitaredomo, Fune ni noborazu.
Mizukara Shôsu, Shin wa, Kore Shuchû no Sen.

Rihaku drank one barrel,
and composed a hundred poems.
Fast asleep at a wine house in Chô-an,
He missed the Emperor's call to meet him aboard ship.
Rihaku calls himself, the drunken Sage.

176

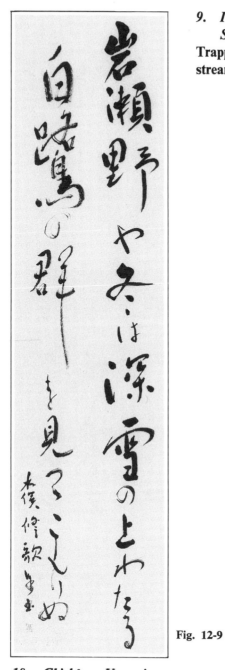

Fig. 12-9

9. *Iwaseno ya, Fuyu wa Miyuki no wataru*
Shirasagi no mure o, Mitsutsu komorinu.
Trapped at home, watching the great white heron
stream across the deep snows of Iwaseno.

Fig. 12-10

10. *Chishô ga Uma ni noru wa*
Fune ni noru ni nitari,
Ganka, I ni ochite, suitei ni nemuru.
Drunk on his horse, Chishô sways like a ship at sea.
Glassy-eyed, if he were to fall into a well,
He'd surely sleep peacefully at the bottom.
        —Toho, *Song of the Eight Drunken Sages*

11. *Kagyû kakujô, Nanigoto o ka Arasou.*
   Sekika, Kôchû Kono mi o yosu.
The nations on the snail's left antenna
Quarrel with those on the right,
While life is just a spark in the flame.
—Hakukyoi, quoting Chuang Tsu on the folly of
human quarrels

Fig. 12-11

Fig. 12-12

12. *Soshin wa Chôsaisu, Shû Butsu no mae,*
   Suichû, O-O-ni shite, Tôzen o aisu.
Soshin is a devout scholar, and a government dignitary
as well. But sometimes he drinks too much, and for-
gets Buddha's teaching.
                    —Toho, *Song of Eight Drunken Sages*

13. *Senri no me o Kiwamen to, Hosshi, sara ni noboru, Issô no rô.*

Wanting to climb ever higher, to see with the eyes of a thousand miles from the highest lookout.

—O-Shikan, Tang Poet

On viewing the magnificent scenery of the sun sinking into the mountains, and the Yellow River sinking into the sea.

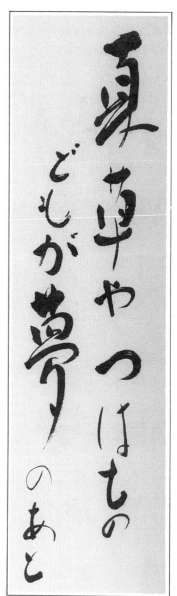

Fig. 12-13

Fig. 12-14

14. *Natsu kusa ya*
    Tsuwa mono domo ga
    Yume no ato.

That young men fought and died on this grassy plain, Seems the aftermath of a dream.

—Bashô, Haiku Poet

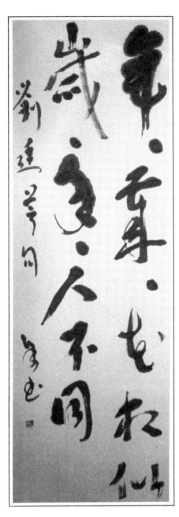

Fig. 12-15

15. *Nen Nen Sai Sai Hana Ai Nitari, Sai Sai*
Nen Nen Hito Onaji Karazu.
Year by year, flowers are over the same. But year
after year, people change.
*awarded "Nyû-sen" prize in 1987 Zen Nitten Exhibition

Fig. 12-16

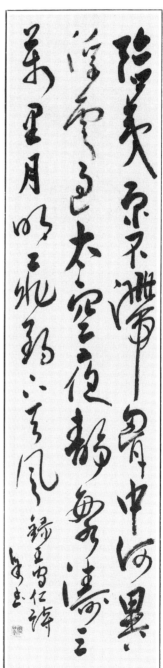

16. *Umi ni Ukabu Ken i moto, Kyôchû ni Todomarazu*
Nan zo Koto Naran,
Fu-un no Tai-kû o Suguru ni Yoru Shizuka ni,
Kaitô San Man Ri
Tsuki Akiraka ni Shaku o Tobashite, Tenpû ni
Kudaru.
ADRIFT
Cast adrift in a turbulent sea,
Where can there anywhere be danger?
Floating on an ocean vast,
You can see for thousands of miles.
The bright moon lights our way,
And rains down its beams on the winds of Heaven.
—O-Shujin, Ming Dynasty poet
*awarded "Toku-sen" prize in 1988 Zen Nitten Exhibition

Shikishi

Fig. 12-17

17.   Ji-gan On-yô.
Have soft eyes, and a gentle manner.
The bow which is always strung may break, and so may the person who never unwinds. A relaxed expression not only endures, it is the strongest.

Fig. 12-18

18.   Tsubo: Tsubo o kata mukete, Yû-shaku o kotoshi.
Vessel of wine: Quietly tilting the flask, drinking in solitude.

—Rihaku

19. *Gukô Yama o Utsusu.*
Gukô moved the mountain.

Gukô was a ninety year old man who lived on the banks of the Yellow River between two mountains. The mountains posed a tremendous obstacle to traffic, so Gukô set out with his son, grandson, and neighbor's son, to transport the mountains by shovelful, and dump them into the ocean. However, a single round trip to the harbor took over a full year, and in light of the old man's age and the seeming impossibility of the plan, the people of the village tried to stop him. Gukô claimed however, that when he died, his sons would carry on, and their sons after him for generations. Since the mountain itself was not growing in size, it was impossible that they could fail to move it.

Fig. 12-19

Fig. 12-20

20. *Ban-yû Ai-go*
Love and protect all creation.

All things are born of a common source, and exist in a common Universe. Therefore we should show them the respect and gratitude that is due.

21. *Intoku Kahô*
Do good in secret, and reward will follow.

During the period of the Chinese Civil Wars, people believed that a person who saw a two-headed snake would surely die within a few days. A young man had just returned from a trip, and his mother found him weeping. She asked what was wrong, and he said that he had seen a two-headed snake, and feared that he would soon die. His mother asked him what he did when he saw the snake, and he replied that he killed and buried it, for fear that others might see it and suffer the same fate as he. His mother told him then that he had nothing to fear, as reward

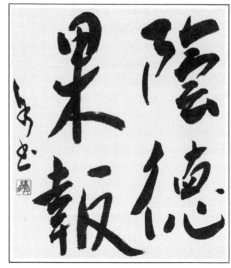

Fig. 12-21

always follows good done in secret. In time he became a great national hero, the protector of many people.

22. *Ware Satori, Hen ni O-zu.*
Wake up and adapt to change.

The word *satori* means enlightenment into the heart of the self. Once you realize your true nature, you no longer attach to vain ideas of a static world. Then you become free and able to adapt to change.

Fig. 12-22

23. *Wakô Dô-jin*
Conceal your light, and live among men.

This saying is attributed to the Taoist philosopher, Lao Tsu. According to Taoist thought, that which is too bright does not last the day, and that which is too sharp soon becomes dull. Therefore we should conceal our strength, and protect our latent talent. To have power, and not display it, requires strength of character. Nevertheless, modesty should conceal strength, not incompetence.

Fig. 12-23

24. *Raku: Tsune ni Shunpû Taitô tare.*
Optimistic: In the spirit of a mild spring breeze.

Ask the people around you what they think of positive thinking. Most will tell you that it is a good idea in principle, but that it does not work very well in practice. What they are really telling you is that they do not understand the principle, and that they have not been successful with it in practice. How do you know if a person has a truly positive attitude? Few people will admit to having a negative attitude. Attitude is as intangible as emotion or thought. We cannot see or measure it directly. Attitudes are not tangible but they are audible, in the words that a person chooses. To paraphrase Oscar Wilde, a pessimist is a person who given the choice of two evils, chooses both. A positive person in the same circumstances will choose something else. Like the glass of water which can be called half-empty or half-full, many things are inherently neutral until we name them. Listen to the language that a person uses to describe his or her free time, salary, or spouse. The quality of our lives is determined more by our attitudes than by our inheritance. Be careful of the company that you keep, because attitude is highly contagious. The negative thinker is a slave of circumstances. It took Confucius seventy years to free his mind from external rules and influences. How long will it take us?

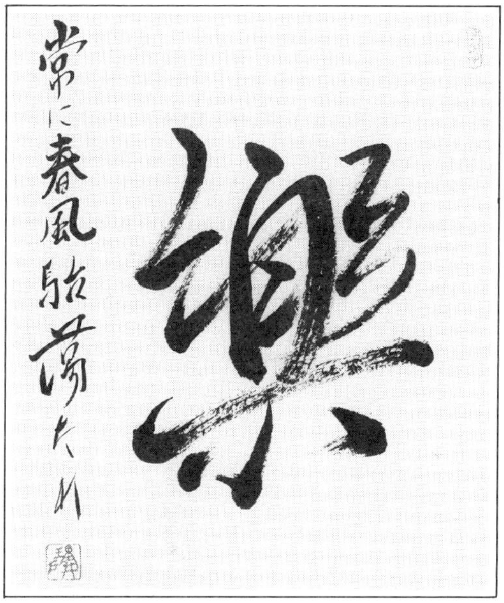

Fig. 12-24

25. *Ichi-go Ichi-e*
One Meeting, One Life.

Samurai warriors readied themselves for battle by shedding their swords and partaking of the Tea Ceremony. The basic assumption of this gathering was that the members assembled may never meet again, and that indeed the occasion itself could never be recaptured. Serenity is found in the intense fulfillment of the moment. We too easily assume that moments can be preserved, on film, tape, or in memory. Do not assume that the ring will always come around again. It may, but if you do not make the most of what you have now, you may find that time and circumstance have put it out of reach.

Fig. 12-25

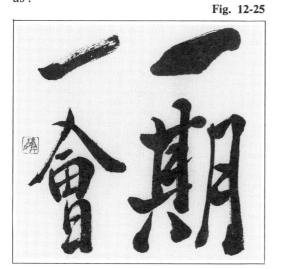

26. *Keizoku wa Chikara Nari.*
Persistence brings power.

Wherever you look, in nature or society, you find that some things endure, while others quickly pass and fade away. Doctors who deal with terminally ill patients recognize the enormous influence of the will to live upon the patient's chances of survival. However patiently a spider may have woven, if its web is destroyed by wind or movement, the spider starts over again and works until it is finished. When you begin training in an art, you see how quickly some people give up, and how quickly those who stay on advance. It is as if we were pushing a cart uphill. As long as we keep pushing, we progress. If we stop, we fall back. The Greek Myth of Syphisus describes a man who is fated to push a rock up to the top of a hill, only to have it roll back down again, forcing him to repeat the process over and over. The existentialists twisted this story with a negative interpretation, saying that life was ultimately futile, and that the only real question was whether or not to commit suicide. However, the real meaning of the story is that continuity is the source of power, and that the alternative is stagnation and death. The source of that power is the Universe itself, which never stops moving or developing. To become one with the Universe is to move, grow, and develop with it. Observe life and the people around you, and draw your own conclusion. To continue, or to regress: in the end, the choice is yours.

Fig. 12-26

27. *Man-sô no Meigetsu*
The bright moon fills
my window.

28. *Shumpû Mono o
Hassu.*
The spring wind
brings all things to
life.

29. *Mukonju*
The tree without roots
  —A Zen expression

30. *Ume no Hayashi*
A plum grove

31. *Hatô*
Crest of the wave

32. *Ki-ichi*
Return to the source

The Principles at a Glance

Chapter 1: Principles for Controlling the Brush
1. Weight forward, Elbow down.
2. Bend Elbow, Not Wrist.
3. Stem Vertical, Fingertips down.
4. Bristles Parallel.
5. Continuous Exhalation.

Chapter 2: Principles for Expressing Energy on Paper
1. Contact the Paper Surface.
2. Use the Free Hand for Support.
3. Accelerate to a Clean Stop.
4. Use Every Hair of the Brush.
5. Maintain Energy on and off the Paper.

Chapter 3: Principles for Giving Dimension to the Flat Surface
1. Saturate the Brush, with Restraint.
2. Minimal Pressure, Maximal Effect.
3. Fast on the Straight, Slow on the Curve.
4. Consider Figure and Ground.
5. Maintain Proper Stroke Angle and Distance.

Chapter 4: Principles for Originality with Excellence
1. Maintain a Spirit of Relaxed Concentration.
2. Expand Your Visual Vocabulary.
3. Be Original, Not Just Different.
4. Find the New in the Old.
5. Link Together What Others Have Not Seen.

Chapter 5: Principles for Visual Literacy
1. Learn the Basic Radicals.
2. Find the Visual Center of Gravity.
3. Picture the Geometric Profile.
4. Learn the Proper Stroke Order.
5. Strive for Visual, Not Verbal Literacy.

Chapter 6: Principles for Image Training and Practice
1. Combine Physical and Mental Rehearsal.
2. Move from the Obvious to the Subtle.
3. Maintain an Unbroken Flow of Ki.

4. Learn How to Read the Score.
5. Refine Your Movements as You Go.

Chapter 7: Principles for Appreciating *Kanji*
1. Study the Development of Script Styles.
2. Appreciate the Rationale of the *Kanji*.
3. Note the Origin of the Phonetic Scripts.
4. Put Etymology in Perspective.
5. Rediscover the Beauty of the Ancient Script.

Chapter 8: Principles for Abbreviated Writing
1. Learn to Read the Abbreviated Hand.
2. In *Gyôsho*: Preserve the Qualities of Character.
3. In *Sôsho*: Maintain the Continuity of the Line.
4. Do Not Sacrifice Legibility.
5. Use Space Generously.

Chapter 9: Principles for Enjoying Calligraphy
1. Respect the Conventions of Mounting and Display.
2. Provide Visual and Verbal Access to the Work.
3. Transfer the Brushwork to Other Media.
4. Develop Original Ideas from Oriental Design.
5. Use Calligraphy to Visualize and Magnify Thought.

Chapter 10: Principles of Design in Japanese Culture
1. Bring the Far Near.
2. Reveal the World within.
3. Find the Unity of Calmness and Action.
4. Seek the Unity of Function and Beauty.
5. Express the Universal in the Particular.

Chapter 11: Principles for Auspicious Handwriting
1. Preserve a Generous Sense of Internal Space.
2. Respect the Regular Intervals between the Strokes.
3. Maintain Good Attitude in Your Written Characters.
4. Avoid Collapse of Enclosed Spaces.
5. Keep the Clarity of the Line Unbroken.

Glossary and Index of Japanese Shodo Terms

192

For Further Study...

There is not a great deal of reliable or useful information available in English on the subject of Shodo. Most of the information in this book was gathered from my own teachers, experience, and extensive reading on the subject in Japanese. What you really need to undertake further study is not more reading, but the materials to paint with, *tehon* from the classical masterpieces, and if possible a teacher.

Materials are usually available, directly or by mail order from a local artist's supply store. If not, you can inquire through the Japan or China Society, University Asian Studies Department, or Embassy/Consulate in your area. Expensive materials are not needed for practice, but you want to be sure to get something better than a toy brush, and handmade paper if available. In this sense, you are better off dealing with a store that specializes in calligraphy supplies.

Most of the classics are well illustrated in academic or museum editions on the subject, but the individual characters are often too small to make good *tehon*. Excellent materials are abundant if you read Japanese or Chinese. It is not easy to find an instructor who is simultaneously a skilled calligrapher, a good teacher, able to speak your language, and geographically accessible. But strangely enough, when your interest is high, you may find that as the student is ready, the teacher appears.

For those seriously interested in pursuing Shodo further by correspondence, the author welcomes letters addressed to Japan Publications, Inc., or c/o:

Reed Research Institute
Tada Bldg. 402 1–9–5 Ebisu, Shibuya-ku, Tokyo 150 Japan
Tel 03–473–2108   Fax 03–473–3108

Index